JORDAN

**His Majesty King Hussein at Jordan's
fiftieth anniversary celebrations**

JORDAN

Arabesque, Amman, Jordan

First published 1978
Ministry of Information, Jordan

Second (revised) edition 1981
© Arabesque

ISBN 0 09 133470 5

Contents

Foreword

Situated at the crossroads of Europe, Asia and Africa, the land of Jordan has been, for eight millenniums, a center of civilization. The great wealth of history and culture appears all over the country, to the extent that Jordan can be considered an immense, open museum. New archaeological sites are ceaselessly discovered, while in the Jordan Rift Valley, near the Dead Sea – lowest point on earth – the visitor can find some of the oldest continuously inhabited settlements in history. Very few changements have occurred there since the times of Moses, of the Edomites, Nabateans and Romans, and the land still has the same harsh beauty of thousands of years ago.

Among the most famous and important sites, Petra and Jerash testify of the ancient splendour, while Amman, the capital, is a busy commercial, economic and cultural centre of 700,000 people, spread over steep hills, crossed by narrow wadis and characterized by the white stone locally used in architecture.

But Jordan, while solidly rooted in the past, is facing the future, a future of development and rapid progress, guided in the last three decades by King Hussein, direct descendent of the Prophet Mohammed, and last in the Hashemite line. Under his guidance, enormous progress has been attained in education, health, welfare, while forward thinking development plans are ensuring economic self-sufficiency. Jordan today relies on an excellent communications system: highways linking neighbouring countries and air, sea and rail routes, all play their role in industrial development.

One of the most hospitable countries in the world for tourists and investors alike, modern Jordan has not forgotten the thousands of years of traditional life in the desert, and heartily considers all visitors honoured guests.

Bas relief from Nineveh depicting a battle with Arabs, c.645 BC. The Arabs are on
camels in pairs. One shoots arrows at the pursuing Assyrian force, while the other
controls the camel with a stick

PART ONE
History

1 The Early Centuries

The antiquities of Jordan have long fascinated archaeologists. For it is likely that somewhere here, on the outermost edge of the Fertile Crescent, in the Jordan Valley, man first abandoned his nomadic way of life in the Early Stone Age and settled down to cultivate crops and to build homes. Around the clusters of these early dwellings grew the first villages to produce an agricultural surplus with which to support civilization and the more complex social organization of a city.

Situated on one of the great crossroads of the world, on the bridgehead between Asia and Africa, the ancient peoples of the area witnessed a long series of conquerors and conquests as powerful empires to their north and south invaded and counter-invaded the land in order to round out their dominions or wrest supremacy from their rivals. In their turn Egyptians, Sumerians, Akkadians, Babylonians, Hittites, Assyrians, Persians, Greeks, Romans, Byzantines and, down to our own day, Arabs, have each made their impact on the country's culture and civilization.

In the early ages, parts at least of east Jordan were submerged beneath the sea; fossilized oysters and other shells have been found in many parts of the country and the phosphate deposits at Ruseifa, to the east, and at Hasa, to the south of Amman, contain the bones and skeletons of hordes of fish, giant lizards and turtles, dating back eighty million years. There were also periods during which the land was subjected to sharp fluctuations in climate; rainfall and fierce volcanic and earthquake activity was constantly changing the contours and appearance of the country.

By the time Paleolithic Man appeared on the scene, about 2 000 000 years ago, physical conditions must have been much as they are now. Typical early paleolithic implements, such as the large, roughly flaked flint hand-axes, have been found all over the country, occasionally in great quantities. Development was slow, and there was little change for about 150 000 years. However, drawings of animals scratched on rock, linked no doubt to primitive religion, are evidence of the growth of artistic talent towards the end of the period.

That human beings should have settled and flourished here is all the more remarkable because of the geographical isolation of the region, and the absence of easily accessible sources of wealth. On the west the river Jordan, the Dead Sea and the Wadi Arabeh effectively separate the East Bank from Palestine; on the east are the great desert wastes, and on the north, where it might have merged into Syria, the gorge of the Wadi Yarmouk makes a natural boundary. On the south the boundary is more open, though the desert-like nature of the country does not make communications particularly easy even today.

Colonnaded street at Petra, second-century AD. Beyond are the Royal Tombs, carved into the western face of the mount of Al Kubtha

In the Neolithic period or New Stone Age (about 8000–4500 BC) progress became much more rapid. Significant recent discoveries reveal that the people used bows and arrows, knew how to make pottery and how to polish the cutting edges of axes. Recent excavations at Jericho and Baidha near Petra have shown that this was a period of far higher culture than previously suspected. Jericho was a settlement of well-built houses with finely plastered floors and walls, surrounded by a great stone wall with a ditch or dry moat, and at least one massive round tower – the oldest known walled city in the world. There is evidence that crops were cultivated and animals domesticated in those parts very early on.

At Baidha a series of villages, each built on the ruins of an earlier one, shows highly sophisticated architectural designs and all kinds of beautifully made flint and bone tools. Neolithic sites of all periods where communal life was fully developed abound in Jordan, some in what is now virtually desert. The use of metal had not yet been discovered and all heavy work, such as stone dressing and rock cutting, was done with hard-stone tools.

In the following Chalcolithic (or Copper) Age (4500–3000 BC) the tempo of development accelerated. Hardly had pottery been evolved when an even more important technique was discovered – the smelting of copper. But early efforts were tentative and flint implements continued to be used in this period.

Excavations at Tulailat Al Ghassul in the Jordan Valley furnish a picture of life in this age, probably about 3500 BC. Here was a village of some size, with well-built houses, some made of sun-dried mud-based bricks on a rough stone foundation, others made entirely of bricks. The roofs were probably of wood, reeds and mud, as are those of many houses in the valley today. The walls of some houses were plastered and painted in bright colours with representations of the human figure, stars and geometrical motifs. The pottery was very advanced and expertly fired; it comprised a varied repertory of shape and decoration, often bearing elaborate geometric designs painted in red or brown. On the bases of some pots were imprints of woven or coiled basketwork; the mat on which vases were made, with pierced circular stones, suggests spindle whorls and weaving. Women adorned themselves with beads of shell and stone, and men, if the paintings are interpreted correctly, were bearded and tattooed. One figure seems to wear a pair of embroidered slippers. Excavations also show that it was a period, at least in the Jordan Valley, of severe earthquakes.

In the Early Bronze Age (3000–2100 BC) – a continuation and development of the Chalcolithic – metal was used in greater quantities and such utilities as swords, daggers and spearheads were made of copper. The Bronze Age is actually something of a misnomer, for in the early and middle periods of this age nearly all the implements that have so far been tested have turned out to be made of copper and not bronze. The designation was adopted in the early days of archaeology, and like many erroneous terms, has not been superseded.

In Jordan, there are many sites dating from this period, from the river Yarmouk in the north to Shobak in the south; and from Bab Al Dhraa on the Lisan of the Dead Sea in the west to Sahab on the edge of the desert to the east; and even as far as Jawa, a small isolated site in the basalt desert near the TAP pipeline pumping station H-5 on the road to Baghdad. The period was prosperous and peaceful, and there were great advances in the arts as well as in purely practical activities. Mining and metalworking were the first specialized industries.

The massive stone tower of Neolithic Jericho, the oldest known walled city in the world, carbon date 6800 BC

12

The Early Bronze Age was brought to an end by an invasion of nomads. Though their culture was much inferior to that of the indigenous Canaanites, they were apparently more warlike, for they captured and destroyed all the principal towns and villages and interrupted the steady cultural growth that had been going on for centuries. But this was only an interlude, for the nomads (thought to be the Amorites) were themselves driven out by a northern invader—the Hyksos or 'Shepherd Kings' of the Bible—who ushered in the Middle Bronze Age proper (2100–1500 BC). These people brought with them a vastly superior culture and, as the country must have been in some confusion, they had no difficulty in establishing themselves and spreading their power as far as Egypt, which they conquered and ruled for almost a century. The Hyksos invaders introduced an entirely new type of pottery, more sophisticated in technique and more beautiful, and the shapes and styles which had prevailed throughout the chalcolithic and early bronze periods gradually disappeared. Luxury goods started to appear, brought largely from Egypt, and one gets the impression of a richer and freer cultural life. In eastern Jordan almost the only remains of the period are pottery and urns found in tombs at Irbid, Amman, Na'ur and Mount Nebo, but further exploration and excavation will no doubt bring more to light.

In the Late Bronze Age (1500–1200 BC) the area around Amman seems to have been a centre for trade from all parts of the Near East, as the temple near Amman Airport suggests. Tombs of the period have been found at Sahab, Madaba and in the Jordan Valley; these also include some early iron age pottery. The presence of sherds characteristic of Mycenaean and Cypriot ware of this time in both tombs and sites shows that the area was well populated and prosperous. This corrects a theory proposed some years ago that, apart from nomadic families, the whole country was unoccupied from about 1900 to 1300 BC. Nomads do not build temples in cities nor do they erect large family vaults for their dead.

The Iron Age (1200–330 BC), which coincides roughly with biblical history, introduced the use of iron for tools and weapons, though bronze was still used for bowls, vases and other utensils, and occasionally for daggers. During this period the country east of the river was divided into three kingdoms: Edom in the south, Moab in the centre and Ammon in the north. Archaeology provides a few brief but interesting glimpses of the beginnings of the period. At Balua, the remains of a Moabite village on the plateau above the Wadi Mujib, was found a stele, a large natural block of basalt, on which is carved an inscription of four lines and three standing human figures. These seem to represent a king flanked by two gods, and everything about them shows strong Egyptian influence, though the workmanship is certainly not Egyptian. The only un-Egyptian features are in the king's headdress and the symbols of the moon and the sun above his shoulders. The inscription is very badly weathered, and the alphabet used cannot be determined definitely, though several attempts have been made to decipher it.

Only one contemporary local account throws light on conditions in the country at that time. This is the 'Moabite Stone', a stele set up by Mesha, King of Moab, in his capital Dhiban in about the middle of the ninth century BC. It describes a war which Mesha had fought against the Israelite Ahab. It is interesting because the names of the towns and villages which he claims to have captured from Ahab can still be identified, and he refers separately to his god Chemosh, to whom he dedicated some of the captured towns.

Stone head of an Ammonite god or king, one of the earliest examples of native sculpture in the round, c.800 BC. The headdress could be either a Syrian cap or a version of the Egyptian crown of Osiris

Pieces of other stelae of about this period have been found at Dhiban and Amman, but they are, alas, no more than tantalizing fragments. They do show, however, that in the main cities records were kept of major events. The discovery of two complete statues and the remains of two others to the north of the Amman Citadel has added considerably to our knowledge of the culture of this period. The style, dress and other details of the figures reflect the influences of the surrounding civilizations–Phoenician, Egyptian and Assyrian. These statues are unique, being the only complete, free-standing figures in the round of this early period, presumably of indigenous workmanship, to be discovered in Jordan or Palestine. They probably date from about 800 BC.

The rise of Assyria as a great military power at the end of the ninth century BC brought changes everywhere, and many of its annals have survived to tell something of Jordan at that time. About 800 BC the country was overrun as far south as Edom, but after a revolt against Assyria, Tiglath Pileser III took the entire country. It is also revealed that the King of Ammon, Samibu, with Chemosh Nadab of Moab and Shalman of Edom, had to pay tribute and submit to control by governors imposed by the conqueror. An attempted revolt in Palestine in 705 BC was not supported east of the Jordan, and in 680 BC, under Esarhaddon, the kings were still paying tribute. A letter to the Assyrian ruler reports, among other things, that the royal governors have brought two mannas of gold from Pudiel of Ammon, one from Musuri of Moab, and about twelve mannas of silver from Qaus-Jaber of Edom.

In the reign of Ashur-bani-pal, who succeeded Esarhaddon in about 650 BC, the Bedouin in the Wadi Sirhan revolted and attacked the vassal kingdoms of Jordan; subsequently the King of the Kedar Arabs was captured by Chemosh

Bas relief from the palace at Nineveh showing Ashur-bani-pal and his queen feasting in a garden, c.645 BC

Haleth, King of Moab. Ammi Nadab was then King of Ammon, and some very interesting tombs of the period have been found to the north of the Amman Citadel, including one containing a seal of 'Adoni Nur servant of Ammi Nadab'. The word 'servant' implied a high court official.

It is at this time that the Assyrian records make the first historical reference to the Nabataeans, later so prominent in Jordan's history, but then occupying the country south and east of Edom, the old land of Midian.

At its height, the Assyrian Empire had conquered Upper Egypt, thus gaining control of the entire Fertile Crescent. Towards the end of the seventh century BC, however, it declined with surprising rapidity, falling prey to an alliance of Scythians, Medes and Babylonians.

During the first half of the sixth century BC the whole Near East was in a state of turmoil. The Kingdom of Babylon inherited the southern portion of the Assyrian Empire, reaching its zenith under Nebuchadnezzar. But Babylonian predominance was to be short-lived, for in 539 BC Cyrus the Great, who had already united Medes and Persians under his rule, took the capital Babylon. The old kingdoms of Egypt, Syria and Mesopotamia were swallowed up by an empire which would endure for two centuries.

Cyrus the Great restored a measure of autonomy to Jordan and Palestine under the satrapy or governorship 'Abar Nahara', that is, beyond the river Euphrates. The Nabataeans in the meantime had been taking over Edom, driving the Edomites into southern Palestine which later became known as Idumea.

After the Persians came the Greeks. Hellenistic culture, introduced by the conquests of Alexander the Great in about 333 BC, spread swiftly in the Near East, and Greek became a second language everywhere. At the death of Alexander his two generals, Ptolemy and Seleucus, divided the Near Eastern empire between them. Their respective dynasties were soon at war with each other, and Jordan found itself sometimes under the Ptolemies, and sometimes under the Seleucids; it was Ptolemy Philadelphus who renamed Amman 'Philadelphia' after himself. During all this time the Nabataeans maintained their independence, and for a while extended their control as far north as Damascus. The Seleucids had tried without success to drive them out of Petra in 311 BC.

Apart from such isolated pockets of independence, the region came successively under the rule of the dominant powers of the time. The Greeks were followed by the Romans. Under the security maintained by the Roman Empire (63 BC to AD 335) Jordan flourished, reaching its peak of prosperity in the second and third centuries AD as the provinces of Syria-Palaestina and Arabia. But under Rome everything was standardized, and the conquered territories virtually ceased to have any individual history of their own. Only mighty nations like Persia could continue to make their mark on history. It was the same under Byzantium (AD 335–636), but with the difference here that the Byzantine Emperors' obsession with matters of doctrine, schism, sects, and the building of pagan temples, caused them rather to forget about the more remote corners of their empire.

Coins of the Seleucid kings Antiochus VI and Tryphon. Minted at Antioch in 144 BC and c.142 BC, each is worth 4 drachmas

At this time a new force was emerging in the Arabian Peninsula. The Prophet Mohammed had succeeded in uniting the Arabs under Islam, and was turning his attention to the two empires of Byzantium and Persia. At Mu'tah, just south of Karak, the first clash between the Muslim Arabs and the Byzantines took place, when a small Muslim force defeated a large and well armed opposing army. In

Nabataean sculpture at Petra. This head, from the Roman period, lies near the Triumphal Arch which spanned the colonnaded street

AD 636, at the decisive battle of Yarmouk, the army of the Byzantine Emperor Heraclius was routed by Caliph Omar, and the Muslims marched on Damascus where eventually the Omayyad caliphs established their capital.

As eastern Jordan lay on the direct route from Syria to Arabia it continued to have some importance, and for a time life was both peaceful and prosperous. But when in the ninth century the Abbasids moved their capital to Baghdad, the area was destined to become a backwater; not on any particular trade route, nor possessing any natural resources, Jordan fell into decay. The country was, however, of sufficient strategic importance in the twelfth century for the Crusaders to occupy part of it and build castles there, notably at Karak (1142) and Shobak

17

The majestic Crusader stronghold of Shobak (Monte Reale), south of the Dead Sea. Renaud de Châtillon actually built ships here and had them transported piecemeal to Aqaba where he launched them on the Red Sea

(Monte Reale, 1115), east and south of the Dead Sea respectively. Ultimately some seven castles were constructed from Karak in the north to Aqaba in the south, to safeguard the south-eastern approaches to the Latin kingdom. Crusader penetration lasted only 100 years though. In 1187 the great Ayyubite Sultan Salah Al Din (Saladin) defeated the Franks at the battle of Hattin. Soon thereafter Ayyubite rule was ended by the Mamelukes, who governed Jordan and Syria till 1516. Then in the sixteenth century the Ottoman Turks began their rule. Their sole concern was with guarding the pilgrim road to Mecca, which followed the route of the country's modern railway.

So Jordan rested, obscure and almost unknown to the Western world, until it revived dramatically to play an important part in the events of the First World War. The remainder belongs to modern history.

2 Glorious Heritage

Continuously inhabited since the dawn of time, Jordan is rich in archaeological sites. So much so, that it is said one can hardly dig a spade into the ground anywhere in the country without unearthing history! The ebb and flow of people and ideas through the ancient Near East, however, has bequeathed to Jordan a heritage more precious than mere antiquities. For in that matrix of ancient cultures were cast the great religious and ethical systems of the West. Beneath the soil and desert sands of Jordan, in the caves and gorges of its mountains, and in the heart of its modern cities, lies evidence of another kind, testimony for pilgrim as well as scholar—Muslim, Christian and Jew alike.

Archaeological exploration continues to reveal new finds every year, and an account of these would require a volume of its own. What follows therefore is a brief description of a few of the country's most famous sites and structures.

Jericho, we have noted, has the distinction of being the oldest walled inhabited city in the world. In an oasis with splendid gardens, Jericho's date palms were a considerable source of revenue. Mark Anthony made a gift of it to Cleopatra, who farmed the land during the reign of King Herod. The modern city (Ariha), forty kilometres north-east of Jerusalem, stands upon the ruins of Crusader and Byzantine settlements.

Among the places of interest in and around Jericho are the Mount of Temptation; and the Omayyad palace at Khirbat Al Mafjar, built probably for the Caliph Hisham Ibn Abd Al Malik (AD 690–743), whose seat was in Damascus and who ruled from 724. Its mosaics and stucco ornaments are a fine example of Omayyad art and architectural design.

The work of the British School of Archaeology at Tall Es Sultan (ancient Jericho) from 1952 to 1958 revealed, amongst other things, the remains of a highly developed and civilized mesolithic (middle stone age) settlement. The most spectacular discovery was the massive circular stone tower, part of the defences of the town, dating back to about 7000 BC. A flight of steps still exists. It was the discovery of these fortifications, together with contemporary houses and other remains, that confirmed Jericho's claim to be the earliest known city in the world.

Remains of an even earlier settlement, going back to about 8000 BC, have also been discovered at the base of the mound; later remains include those of the mud-brick town walls of the early bronze age city (about 3000–2100 BC) and houses and streets of the Canaanite city (Middle Bronze Age, about 1900–1600 BC).

Near Jericho are the northern shores of the Dead Sea, and the plateau of Khirbat Qumran, in whose caves the famous Dead Sea Scrolls were discovered

Interior of the Dome of the Rock, Jerusalem. The great rock Al Sakhra is venerated by Muslims as the site of the Prophet's ascension to heaven

21

by chance in 1947. A considerable number of fragments was put on public display at the time, but examination of the scrolls is now restricted to scholars.

Like almost every centre of population in Jordan the capital, Amman, is both ancient and modern. Three thousand years ago it was Rabath Ammon, capital city of the Ammonites, a tough little nation which fought long to retain its independence. Under the Ptolemies it was renamed Philadelphia, after reconstruction by its conqueror, Ptolemy Philadelphus. In 63 BC it joined the Decapolis, a league of free Greek cities strung along the caravan routes of the time which banded together for protection.

Many of the city's antiquities, such as the Acropolis, were destroyed in the Middle Ages; others survived till comparatively recent times. But a remarkable Roman monument remains: the great theatre built against a natural recess in one of the seven hills on which Amman stands. The theatre was large enough to accommodate 8000 spectators. It is still used for concerts and other performances. Another survival is the Citadel, which includes a Roman temple to Hercules and a seventh-century Arab fortress. The museum nearby contains many of the finds from excavations in and around the city. On Citadel Hill archaeologists have found quantities of middle bronze age objects dating back to the sixteenth century BC.

The caves at Khirbat Qumran where the Dead Sea Scrolls were discovered
Left : Date palms and bananas in sub-tropical Jericho

Qasr Al Kharana,
Omayyad fortress and
hunting lodge south-
east of Amman

Among the less widely known, but certainly most fascinating, Muslim treasures are the Desert Castles, a string of palaces built by the Omayyad caliphs in the seventh and eighth centuries AD. There are six of these: Mushatta, Kharana, Muwaggar, Amra and Tuba in east Jordan, and Khirbat Al Mafjar at Jericho in Palestine. The caliphs, who were based in Damascus, were skilled horsemen and keen hunters, and they built these palaces to serve as hunting lodges. They were luxurious rest houses, containing well-appointed living quarters for the caliphs and their families, a heated bath, a fountain in an open courtyard and space for horses and servants; they also included a mosque with *mihrab* (altar) and a fortified tower.

Some of the palaces, notably Khirbat Al Mafjar, have beautiful mosaics. Qasr Amra is the best preserved, with fine frescoes and mosaic floors. Decorative carvings reflect the lives and pleasures of the occupants. The only one of these buildings obviously constructed as a fortress is the massive four-square Qasr Al Kharana.

One of the most spectacular of Jordan's ancient monuments is the Roman city at Gerasa, now known as Jerash. Its antiquities are numerous enough and sufficiently well preserved to show how luxuriously its inhabitants lived in the centuries immediately preceding and following the start of the Christian era. The great oval forum outlined with dome columns and approached by what is now

23

Roman amphitheatre at Jerash and beyond, the forum, approached by the Street of the Columns

called the Street of Columns was the centre of social activity. There were two public baths, three theatres, and a hippodrome; a Nymphaeum, which is a complex of fountains and sculptures; a triumphal arch in honour of Hadrian; and perhaps most striking of all, the Temple of Artemis.

Jerash flourished during the first and second centuries BC. In 63 BC the city and its lands were annexed by Pompey to the province of Arabia. However, early in the Roman period of its history Jerash joined the Decapolis, the League of Free Cities. At this time it had a flourishing trade with the Nabataeans and many of their coins and architectural remains have been found there.

In AD 90 Jerash was absorbed anew into a Roman province, and began a period of great prosperity and rebuilding. The Street of Columns, the two streets crossing it at the North and South Tetrapylons and many of the monuments, which are still standing, were built during this period with the help of gifts from wealthy citizens, who seem to have taken pride in contributing to the embellishment of their town.

The visit of the Emperor Hadrian to the city in AD 129–30 was the signal for a renewal of building activity, including the commemorative Triumphal Arch. This was the golden age of Jerash.

The Persian invasion of 614 marked the beginning of its decline. During the Crusader period, the Atabek of Damascus converted the Temple of Artemis into a fortress, which was destroyed by Baldwin II (1118–31). Jerash then sank into oblivion until its eastern half was occupied by Circassians in 1878. It had in fact almost disappeared from view under the desert sands, and it was not till excavations began early in the twentieth century that the world learnt how much of the Roman provincial glory still remained.

More remarkable even than Jerash is Petra, known in the Bible and old Arab literature as 'Sela' or Rock Cleft. Multi-coloured, mysterious and of breathtaking beauty, Petra was a lost and legendary city until it was rediscovered by a young Swiss explorer called John Burkhardt in 1812. He came upon a narrow

The only access to the hidden city of Petra is along the Siq, a winding, thread-like trail between twin escarpments 65 metres high

Byzantine mosaic map of Jerusalem at Madaba, possibly the oldest map of the Holy City in existence

gorge between vertical cliffs, and emerging on the other side saw the remains of a city-fortress cut into sheer rock. There was a columned street, an amphitheatre, tombs, sculptures, a gigantic monastery, and, most spectacular of all, the Treasury, its façade carved in the rock face, almost untouched by the centuries.

Petra was the stronghold of the Nabataeans, first heard of as nomads roaming the North Arabian desert in the sixth century BC. From their hidden and powerfully defended metropolis they held potential conquerors at bay for generations. The Nabataeans succumbed finally to the Romans under Trajan in AD 105, when the source of their water was discovered and the supply cut. They prospered under Rome, engaged in the caravan trade and used their wealth to enlarge and beautify their unique city.

This prosperity was, however, short-lived, and in the third century AD decline set in. This was caused mainly by the abandonment of the land route of the Arabian caravans in favour of the easier route by the Red Sea, and also by the rise of a rival city, Palmyra, in the north.

Christianity came to Petra during the fourth and fifth centuries, and some of the largest buildings, particularly the great monastery of Ad Deir, were cleared and converted into churches.

Gradually Petra deteriorated. By the time of the Arab conquest in the seventh century it was a dead city, and before long even the memory of Petra was lost to all but a few Bedouin, who jealously guarded the secret of its location until its discovery by the intrepid explorer.

Among other antiquities the mosaics of Madaba are worth special mention. Many are in the town's museum, but the most remarkable of all, dating from the sixth century AD, is preserved in the Greek Orthodox church. It is a mosaic map of Jerusalem, so clear and accurate that many of the buildings can readily be identified.

26

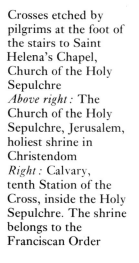

Crosses etched by pilgrims at the foot of the stairs to Saint Helena's Chapel, Church of the Holy Sepulchre

Above right: The Church of the Holy Sepulchre, Jerusalem, holiest shrine in Christendom

Right: Calvary, tenth Station of the Cross, inside the Holy Sepulchre. The shrine belongs to the Franciscan Order

Near Madaba is Mount Nebo, from the summit of which Moses is said to have looked across the river Jordan to the land of Canaan. According to some legends he is buried on the mountain. Nearby is Syagha, where there is a church and a monastery with fine mosaics dating back to the sixth century.

As the land of the Bible, Jordan is exceptionally blessed in the number and concentration of its holy sites and memories. Across the centuries the faithful of the three great monotheistic religions have made their way here to follow in the steps of the prophets, or visit the scenes of Christ's ministry. Every foot of the country has a familiar story to tell, and clearly it is possible here only to indicate those major points of pilgrimage.

For Christians, the sanctuaries of Jerusalem are held in deepest reverence. The Church of the Holy Sepulchre in the heart of the Old City was originally built by the Roman Emperor Constantine (c. 280–337), but the present building dates back to Crusader times. The holiest shrine in Christendom, it is built upon the traditional site of the Crucifixion around the Hill of Golgotha (Calvary). It also marks the place where Constantine's mother, St Helena, is reputed to have found the True Cross.

The church belongs to six communities, each with definite rights. Three are major: Greek Orthodox, Armenian and Roman Catholic. They have effective residence and individual chapels. The three minor communities are the Syrian (Jacobite), the Coptic and Abyssinian. The rights of each community are determined by the arrangement known as the Status Quo of 1852.

The Church of St Anne stands on the traditional site where the Virgin's parents, Anne and Joachim, are believed to have lived at the time of her birth. Consecrated in 1140 by Yvette, daughter of Baldwin II, it is one of the finest examples of Crusader architecture in the Holy Land. Within the precincts of the White Fathers is the Pool of Bethesda, where Jesus healed the man 'who had an infirmity for thirty-eight years'.

Equal in sanctity with the shrines of Jerusalem are those of Bethlehem—the focal point of Christendom at Christmas time.

Towering above all else in Bethlehem is the ancient Church of the Nativity. From early Christian times, the simple cave, the Grotto of the Nativity, has been revered as the birthplace of Jesus. The church was originally built in 330 by St Helena. It was damaged by the Samaritans in 521, but the Emperor Justinian had it repaired and the splendid pillars erected. Fortunately the invading Persians spared it, and the present building is therefore an inheritance from Justinian and before him the pious Queen Helena. The church is jointly shared by the Roman Catholic, Greek Orthodox and Armenian communities.

Other Christian holy places in Jordan mentioned in the New Testament are the Field of Shepherds, Bethphage, Bethany, where Lazarus and his two sisters lived, the river Jordan itself, where Jesus was baptized by John, Jericho, where He passed on His way to Jerusalem spending a day in the house of Zacheus, the Mount of Temptation, and Emmaus.

To Muslims, Jerusalem is the third Holy City on earth, after Mecca and Medina in the Hejaz. All Palestine and Jordan have been Muslim Arab countries since the early years of the seventh century, when they served as a springboard for

Shrine in the Church of
the Nativity, Bethlehem

the establishment of Islam beyond the Arabian Peninsula. Many mosques and
shrines in Jerusalem were originally built to commemorate Muslim martyrs, or
sahabah (friends of the Prophet Mohammed), who died here while fighting the
Byzantine armies.

Al Haram Esh Sharif, the Noble Sanctuary, is the name given to the compound
containing the Mosque of Al Aqsa and the Dome of the Rock. This enclosure,
sacred to the Muslims, is situated on Mount Moriah within the walled city of
Jerusalem.

The Rock is mentioned in the Koran, where it is associated with the Prophet
Mohammed's nocturnal visit to Jerusalem and his ascension to Heaven. As the
site of the Prophet's ascension it is the first *qiblah* in Islam (the point towards
which Muslims turn in prayer). Jerusalem and its Rock acquired early sanctity in
Muslim eyes, and when the Caliph Omar Ibn Al Khattab entered Jerusalem in
637, he helped clear, with his own hands, the accumulated refuse of centuries,
and had a simple mosque of wood built upon Moriah. The present Dome of the
Rock was built by the Omayyad Caliph Abdul Malik Ibn Marwan in 691. It is
a magnificent example of Muslim architecture, and is considered among the most
beautiful monuments in the world.

Repair work on the Dome of the Rock and Al Aqsa mosques was started in
1956. The lead dome was removed together with its wooden supports and replaced
by another made of aluminium covered with a layer of gold.

In addition to the Dome of the Rock, the Al Haram Esh Sharif area includes
the Mosque of Al Aqsa to the south, built by the Caliph Walid I; the underground
vaults, known as Solomon's Stables; as well as smaller domes, minarets, fountains,
shrines, a library and a museum.

Al Aqsa's exquisite *minbar* (pulpit) of elaborately carved cedar wood, gilded and
inset with ivory, which was built by Salah Al Din in the thirteenth century, was
burned down under the Israelis in 1969.

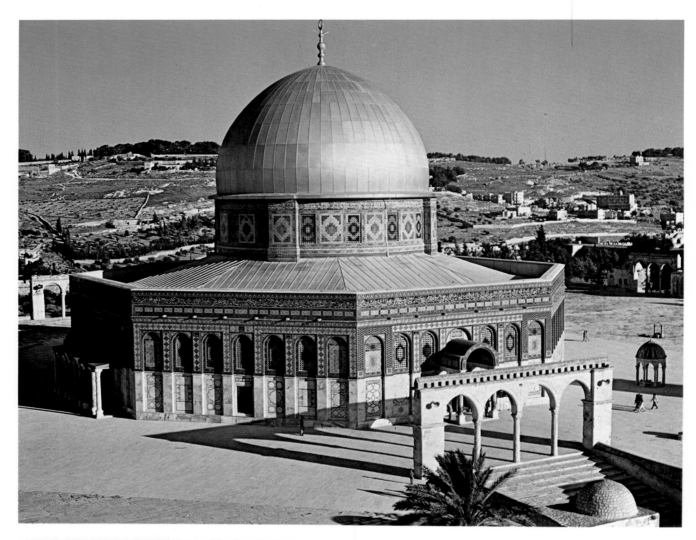

The magnificent Omayyad
Dome of the Rock in the
Haram compound

Left: Arched pillars and
ceiling in the Mosque of Al
Aqsa, Jerusalem

At Hebron, the mosque of Al Haram Al Ibrahimi incorporates the Grotto of Machpela, where Abraham, his wife Sarah, Isaac, Rebecca, Leah and Jacob lie buried. The mosque is of great architectural interest and of exceptional importance because Ibrahim Al Khalil, 'The Friend of God', is venerated by Muslims as the first Prophet.

The small village of Mazar, nine miles to the south of Kerak, has a famous mosque with two domes and two tall minarets, built over the tomb of Ja'afar Ibn Abu Talib, cousin of the Prophet Mohammed, killed in AD 629 in the first battle between Muslim and Byzantine armies. Nearby are two more domes built over the tombs of two leaders who fell in the same battle.

The Jordan Valley has several domes and tombs built to commemorate Muslim leaders, the most famous being that of the great general Abu Obeidah, companion of the Prophet. Jordan has many mosques: there is hardly a village without one. In Amman and district alone there are 180 mosques, with about 200 more under construction.

Building on the past. The Roman amphitheatre in the centre of modern Amman has been carefully restored and is used today for concerts and contemporary drama

PART TWO
The Emergence
Modern Jordan

The Royal Family

**Hashemite Branch
of the Prophet's Descendants**

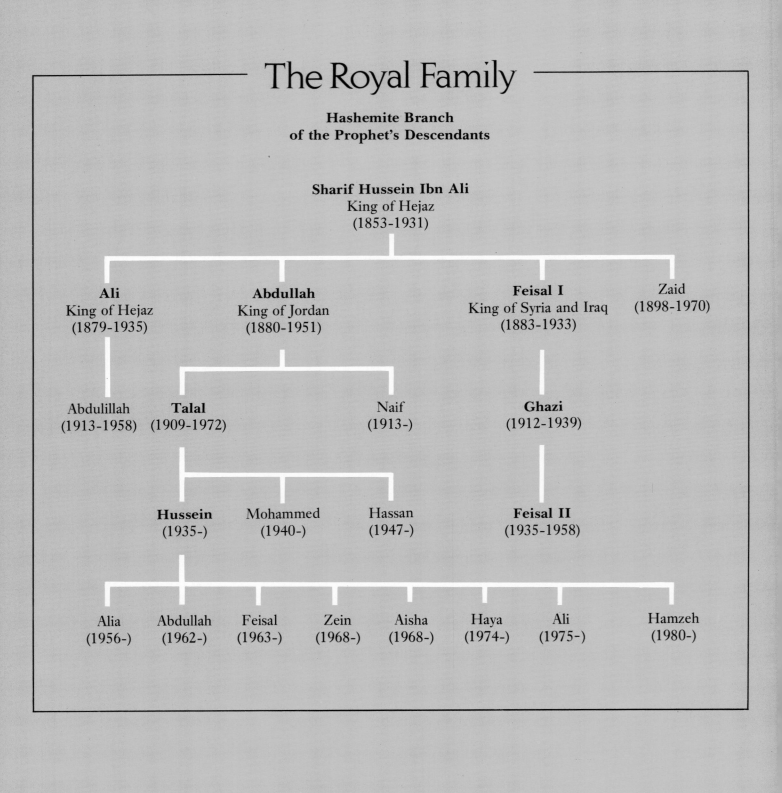

Sharif Hussein Ibn Ali
King of Hejaz
(1853-1931)

Ali
King of Hejaz
(1879-1935)

Abdullah
King of Jordan
(1880-1951)

Feisal I
King of Syria and Iraq
(1883-1933)

Zaid
(1898-1970)

Abdulillah
(1913-1958)

Talal
(1909-1972)

Naif
(1913-)

Ghazi
(1912-1939)

Hussein
(1935-)

Mohammed
(1940-)

Hassan
(1947-)

Feisal II
(1935-1958)

Alia
(1956-)

Abdullah
(1962-)

Feisal
(1963-)

Zein
(1968-)

Aisha
(1968-)

Haya
(1974-)

Ali
(1975-)

Hamzeh
(1980-)

3 The Hashemites

Hussein Ibn Talal, thirty-ninth in the line of descent from the Prophet Mohammed

The history of modern Jordan is synonymous with that of its founding dynasty, the Hashemites. The Hashemites are so called after the great-grandfather of the Prophet Mohammed, who belonged to the noblest Arab tribe, the Quraish of Mecca. They are descended in the male line from Mohammed's daughter Fatima. She had two sons: Hassan, whose descendants have been known as Ashraf (Arabic plural of Sharif–'Honourable'), and Hussein, ancestor of the Asyad (plural of Sayyed–'Master'). King Hussein of Jordan is of the line of Ashraf, for centuries lords of the Hejaz, in the heart of the Arabian Peninsula, and guardians of the holy cities of Mecca and Medina. He is thirty-ninth in the direct line of descent from the Prophet.

The Sharifian House of Aoun, to which King Hussein belongs, came to prominence during the first half of the nineteenth century. Its founder, Mohammed Ibn Aoun, was for twenty-seven years the Amir (Prince) of Mecca, whose jurisdiction spread throughout the Hejaz. His sons and grandsons ruled in Mecca for nearly a century, between 1827 and 1925.

The Grand Sharif Hussein Ibn Ali (1853–1931), was accorded the title Al Munquiz Al A'zam, 'the Grand Saviour', in the Arab world following his leadership of the Great Arab Revolt against the Ottoman Empire in 1916. His four sons, Ali (1879–1935), Abdullah (1880–1951), Feisal (1883–1933) and Zaid (1898–1970), provided the practical and executive leadership of the Arab independence movement in its most important and critical phase, during the First World War and in the wake of the Versailles Treaty of 1922.

Ali succeeded Hussein as King of the Hejaz (1924–5). His son Abdulillah and daughter Aliyah were instrumental in maintaining stability during the Regency in Iraq. Feisal, after confronting the French in Syria, became King of an independent Iraq. He was succeeded by his son Ghazi (1912–39), who married his cousin Aliyah. On Ghazi's death his son, Feisal II (1935–58), was only three and so the Regency fell upon Abdulillah until 1953 when Feisal came of age.

In 1921 Abdullah established the Amirate of Jordan. He was succeeded in 1951 by his eldest son, Talal (1909–72), but illness tragically cut short the latter's reign. Thus on 11 August 1952 the crown of Jordan devolved upon his son, the seventeen-year-old Amir Hussein. As he was not yet of age a Regency Council was elected to govern the country until 2 May 1953 when, according to the Muslim Lunar Calendar, the young King attained his majority.

Hashemite initiative, skill and endurance have played a crucial role in shaping the fortunes of the Arab world. Nowhere is this better illustrated than in the tangled skein of events which comprise the recent history of Jordan.

4 Recent History

The Hashemite Kingdom of Jordan is one of several states which came into being as a result of the First World War (1914–18). For four centuries before the conclusion of that conflict, all the Arab countries of Asia had formed part of the Ottoman Empire, the Sultan of which was the Muslim Caliph–both king and spiritual leader. Being mostly Muslim, therefore, the Arabs felt some satisfaction in paying allegiance to the only Muslim power of the time. They attained high positions in the civil service and the army, not as Arabs, but as Ottomans with a Turkish education. Under the Ottoman constitution, the Arab countries were represented both in the Senate and the House of Representatives. In general, the Arabs were a sort of partner in the State and their condition was not much worse than that of the majority of the Turks themselves.

The great grandfather of King Hussein, Sharif Hussein Ibn Ali, was a man of strong character and independent views. He had expressed his disapproval of the way in which the people of the Hejaz were being treated by the Turks and consequently the Sultan, Abdul Hamid II, 'invited' him to live in Istanbul–an honorary forced exile. Sharif Hussein remained in the Turkish capital for sixteen years with his family and four sons. The turning point came in 1908 when the Sultan appointed him Amir (Prince) of Mecca.

In that year, 1908, there was a revolution in Turkey. The authority of the Sultan-Caliph was drastically reduced and the party of the 'Young Turks', the Committee of Union and Progress, came to power. Under their aegis the former pan-Islamic policies of inter-communal co-operation were abandoned for more exclusive notions of Turkish nationalism or 'Turkism'. Laws were passed giving the Turkish race supremacy and control throughout the Empire. The Arabs were especially aggrieved at the regulations which stipulated that Turkish should be the only official language in their lands. Arab intellectuals and leaders reacted angrily. Secret societies sprang up in protest within the Empire and abroad. Initially, however, the Arab national movement did not entertain the idea of separation. It called for reform and a share in the governing of Arab lands.

Sharif Hussein, by his strong will and personality and great capacity for work, was able to establish himself as the natural spokesman for the Arabs. Almost from the moment he became Amir he was active, sometimes openly, sometimes discreetly, in the movement for Arab sovereignty. He both curbed the authority of his official partner in the Hejaz, the Ottoman Wali, and proved his leadership there by sending expeditions eastwards into Nejd to subdue insurgent tribes. He led a successful campaign to the southern province of Assir, where a local Amir had rebelled, and was able to relieve the besieged garrison. In his military

Men of the Desert Patrol of the Jordan Arab Army

operations and in the work of administration he was assisted by his three eldest sons, Zaid being but a boy at the time.

Hussein had good connections in the Ottoman capital itself and was able to keep informed of trends and developments. His brother, Sharif Nasser, was a member of the Ottoman Senate and his sons Abdullah and Feisal represented the Hejaz in the House of Representatives. Through them he was in constant touch with the Arab parliamentary bloc, which constituted an Arab revolutionary party, formed to defend the rights of all the Arab provinces. This bloc included in its membership prominent Arabs from Syria, Iraq, the Hejaz and Yemen, and looked to the Grand Sharif for leadership. When in 1914 the Young Turks sought his opinion about participation in the war, he strongly advised against it. A new Wali was sent to curb the power of the Sharif, but Hussein was able to outmanoeuvre him.

Not long before the Ottoman Empire became involved in the First World War, Sharif Hussein was approached from three directions. The Ottomans wanted him to send a volunteer force to join the attack on the Suez Canal against the Entente powers; the Arab nationalist movement urged him to assume the mantle of its leadership because of the personal prestige which his family descent conferred upon him; and the British were trying to win him to the Allied cause in exchange for their support of independence for the Arab countries of Asia (excluding Aden).

Sharif Hussein Ibn Ali, author of the Great Arab Revolt

For some months, the Sharif considered these alternatives. A number of events and factors influenced his final decision. In the first place, there was the oppressive policy imposed by the Turks in Syria, where several intellectuals and leaders were hanged, which intensified in the Arabs the spirit to revolt. The outbreak of the Great War had changed the demands for reform to an all-out cry for Arab unity and independence. Moreover the Caliph had instructed him to declare a *jihad* (holy war) from Mecca against the Allies, thus giving Turkey's pro-German involvement a spiritual cachet. However, in June 1916, on the strength of British pledges, Sharif Hussein declared the Arab Revolt at a mass rally in Mecca. Feisal and Ali were poised at Medina, Abdullah at Taif. Shortly thereafter, regular and irregular Arab troops flocked to join the uprising all the way from Mecca in the south to Aleppo in the north. On 2 November 1916 the nobility of Mecca met in conclave to bestow upon Sharif Hussein the title of King of the Arab Countries.

In July 1917, the Arab army captured the port of Aqaba, eventually extending its operations into Transjordan, Palestine and Syria, on the eastern flank of General Allenby's forces. On 1 October 1918, Arab troops entered Damascus alongside the British armies. The Allies recognized the Arabs as belligerents and an Arab administration was established under Feisal, as Viceroy to the Grand Sharif, in present day Syria and Transjordan.

The end of the war, however, brought disillusionment. By the terms of the secret Sykes-Picot agreement Great Britain and France had divided the Sultan's former dominions between themselves into spheres of influence. The Balfour Declaration of 1917 pledged the establishment of a national home for the Jews in Palestine. In the protracted negotiations at the Paris Peace Conference, the great powers were proving more concerned with curbing each other's pretensions than with recognizing Arab aspirations.

Sensing the general drift of things, the nationalist leaders evolved their own solution. On 8 March 1920, the General Syrian Congress meeting in Damascus announced the full independence of Syria, including Palestine, and proclaimed Feisal constitutional monarch of the United Kingdom of Syria. At the same time another proclamation was made, declaring the independence of Iraq under the kingship of Abdullah.

Great Britain and France did not recognize the independence declarations; the Allied Supreme Council took immediate measures to conclude the San Remo Agreement, by which the assignment of mandates to Britain (Iraq, Palestine) and France (Syria, Lebanon) was fixed.

Not long thereafter, the French military governor in the Lebanon submitted an ultimatum to Feisal, which was followed by the advance of French troops on Damascus. After several days' fighting Damascus was occupied. Feisal was dethroned and asked to leave the country, and French claims in Syria were finally established by force of arms.

The fall of the Arab State in Syria was a great blow to Arab aspirations. Sharif Hussein, now King of the Hejaz, was greatly disturbed by the turn of events and he refused to sign a treaty with Britain endorsing the mandate system. He never accepted the Balfour Declaration. Hopes were revived, however, when he received appeals from Syria and Transjordan in which the people announced their readiness to resist the invaders, anticipated his help and invited one of his sons to lead them in their struggle.

Accordingly Abdullah set off across the desert from Medina. The choice was wise since Amir Abdullah had played an active role in the Great Arab Revolt. He had commanded the Eastern Army, which captured Taif and Medina. After 1918, he held the post of Minister for Foreign Affairs in the Hejaz and, in March 1920, the General Congress in Damascus had demonstrated its confidence in him by proclaiming him King of Iraq.

Abdullah reached Ma'an (then administered by the Hejaz) at the head of a combined force of regulars and irregulars, and, proclaiming his intention of marching upon Damascus and restoring Feisal to his throne, urged the Syrians to rally to him and rise up in rebellion. Disturbed, the French asked their British allies to find a way to send the Amir back to the Hejaz. The British warned Abdullah that they would not allow the territory under their Mandate (i.e. Transjordan) to be a base for operations against the French and advised him to leave Ma'an; but Abdullah insisted that he was on Hejazi territory.

The response to the Amir's arrival, however, was not as effective as he had expected. He had insufficient men, weapons and funds for a march against the French, and the Syrians were subdued under tightened French control. The Transjordanian reaction was more positive and encouraging.

Transjordan was the only part of the geographical entity known at that time as Syria which was not occupied by European military forces. Although Great Britain included it in her Mandate, she had not incorporated the area into the Palestine administration, and had appointed only a few political officers to help establish local administrations in the three districts of the country: Irbid, Salt and Karak. These administrations, formed in September 1920, proved too weak to impose their authority. Exiled Syrian patriots assiduously helped spread the Amir's cause among the Transjordanian population.

At this point the British government decided to come to an understanding with the Arabs. They invited Feisal to London for political discussions, insisting,

Amir Abdullah Ibn
Hussein, founder of the
Hashemite Kingdom of
Jordan

however, that Amir Abdullah should not take any further action pending the outcome.

But the enthusiasm of the Transjordanians for the cause of Arab independence culminated in meetings of the people, and in the sending of delegations to Ma'an inviting Abdullah to proceed northwards. Thus, after a sojourn of almost four months at Ma'an, the Amir arrived at Amman on 2 March 1921. He was received by delegations from all over the country offering their allegiance.

In the meantime, Mr Winston Churchill, the British Minister for the Colonies, had convened a conference in Cairo to try to find solutions to the problems of the Middle East. By way of compromise, the conference decided to offer Amir Feisal the throne of Iraq, under a British Mandate. At first it was decided to occupy Transjordan militarily, but Churchill had second thoughts when he received a letter from Abdullah expressing the Arab viewpoint.

Churchill invited Abdullah to meet him in Jerusalem. Four meetings were held towards the end of March 1921, in which the Amir tried to persuade Churchill that the best course would be to constitute Palestine and Transjordan as a single state under an Arab prince. Churchill insisted that the British government would not change its declared policy with regard to Palestine, but in the end suggested that Amir Abdullah himself remain in Transjordan and take charge of its administration. An agreement was reached between the two men on the following lines:

1. The establishment of a national government in Transjordan, headed by Amir Abdullah.
2. The government would have complete administrative independence.
3. A British resident would be appointed in Amman to represent the Mandatory Power.
4. Great Britain would give financial support to Transjordan.
5. Transjordan would not be used as a base for attacks on Syria or Palestine.
6. Great Britain would maintain an airport in Amman.

During the discussions, Churchill pointed out that a policy of reconciliation with the French might lead to the instatement of Abdullah in Damascus as Amir of Syria. He promised that his government 'would do everything that they could to attain this objective'. In the meantime, Churchill arranged for the modification of the Mandate terms to exclude Transjordan from the application of the clauses relating to the creation of a Jewish national home in Palestine.

The Amir Feisal, meanwhile, proceeded in the summer of 1921 to Iraq, where a plebiscite was held. His candidature for the Iraqi throne obtained an enormous majority of the suffrage, and he was formally proclaimed King of Iraq on 23 August 1921. The country attained full independence in 1932, but Hashemite rule there came to an end in July 1958 when a military *coup d'état* ended the government of King Feisal II.

Sharif Hussein, author of the Great Arab Revolt, never saw his dream of a united Arab state realized. On the contrary, repeated attacks on the Hejaz by the fundamentalist Wahhabis from the Nejd obliged him to abdicate in favour of his son Ali in 1924. The great man sought refuge in Cyprus, and ended his days in Abdullah's palace in Amman in 1931. He is buried in the Aqsa Mosque in Jerusalem.

For over a year Ali defended his country with dogged courage, but to no avail, and in December 1925 he too surrendered office. For the first time since the twelfth century there was no Hashemite guardian of the Holy Places.

To the north of the Arabian Peninsula the Hashemite tree had firmly taken root. Amir Abdullah began his rule by unifying the three districts of Transjordan. He selected Amman as his seat of government because it was on the railway, then the only means of mechanical transportation in the country. On 11 April 1921 the first Council of Ministers was formed and work was started on establishing the various departments of a central administration.

The new state had little to build on. The country was poor and backward. The people were mainly farmers and Bedouin. The Amir himself had to take up residence in tents on the hill of Marka. There were neither paved roads, nor water systems, electricity or telephones. Educated and experienced personnel were few, and the Council of Ministers had only one Jordanian member. Most of the British financial grant was expended on a small military force, formed to keep order in the country, the Arab Legion, which was commanded by a British officer.

At first the government had difficulty in keeping order. During the second month after its formation, the Legion attempted to subdue some villagers in the north who were refusing to pay their taxes, but it encountered spirited resistance and was defeated with heavy losses. The government had to wait a year to increase the number of troops and assert its authority. There were difficulties also with the French when Syrian nationalists who had taken refuge in Transjordan made a number of sorties across the frontier, including an attack on the High Commissioner, General Gouraud. The French were intent on ruling Syria, and in the face of their overwhelming military power Amir Abdullah had to abandon the idea of Syria's reunification with Transjordan.

International recognition was obtained when the League of Nations approved, on 23 September 1922, a British memorandum excepting Transjordan from the application of the Jewish national home clauses in the Mandate for Palestine. This was followed on 25 May 1923 by British official recognition of Transjordan's independence.

The final stage in the establishment of the Amirate was the incorporation, in June 1925, of the southern regions of Ma'an and Aqaba. These districts used to form part of the Hejaz, but during the war with the Saudis, King Ali, brother of Abdullah, renounced them in favour of Transjordan.

Slowly but surely the young state progressed, building roads, schools, hospitals and clinics. Security and peace soon ceased to be an issue. The Bedouin were encouraged to settle and the farmers to use better methods. Newspapers and magazines were published in Amman for the first time. Young men began to graduate and take positions of responsibility in the government service.

Transjordan's relations with Great Britain were formalized by the conclusion of a treaty on 20 February 1928. Following this, an Organic Law was enacted and a Legislative Council elected. In spite of its harsh terms, the treaty was ratified by the Legislative Council on 4 June 1929.

The administration of Transjordan was now firmly established, except in parts of the desert region inhabited by Bedouin tribes.

Strife was endemic among the Bedouin, who also exchanged raids with tribes from Central Arabia. A Desert Patrol, composed of Bedouin tribesmen, was formed in 1930 under the command of Captain John Bagot Glubb. With the help of wireless, armoured cars and a number of fortified posts, this force was able to bring peace to the desert for the first time in centuries. During the Second World War, the Desert Patrol was enlarged to become the Mechanized Regiment of the Arab Legion, which developed into the Jordan Arab Army.

The treaty with Great Britain was modified in the interest of Transjordan in 1934, and again in 1939. The clauses restricting the expansion of the army were abolished, and Amir Abdullah was given the right to appoint diplomatic representatives to the neighbouring Arab countries.

When the Second World War broke out in 1939 the Amir did not falter in his alliance with Great Britain. He declared his country's adherence to the cause of the Allies. Transjordan became an important communications link between the countries of the Middle East, and the Arab Legion participated actively in military operations in Iraq and Syria; its units were also detailed to guard bridges, ports, railways, depots and oil pipelines from Cairo in the west to Teheran in the east. Though only 8000 strong, the Legion was the only Middle Eastern force that actively contributed to the Allied war effort.

Towards the end of the war, Transjordan was among the original seven Arab states which, on 22 March 1945, formed the League of Arab States.

The unequivocal stand of Transjordan during the war provided a new basis for relations with Great Britain. Thus, on 22 March 1946, a treaty of alliance and friendship was signed between the two countries, in accordance with which the Mandate was abolished and full sovereignty attained. A military protocol attached to the treaty gave Britain the right to station troops in Jordan, while Britain agreed to offer financial and military aid to Jordan and British officers were to serve in the Jordanian army and help in its training.

As a result the Amirate became the Hashemite Kingdom of Jordan and on 25 May 1946 the Legislative Council proclaimed King Abdullah a constitutional monarch. This date has since become Jordan's independence day.

Not long after the war, a challenging problem faced Jordan and the Arab world. There was strife and bloodshed in Palestine between the Arabs, the original inhabitants of the country, and the Jews who had immigrated there under British auspices. Various solutions were attempted but failed, until in November 1947 Great Britain declared it would no longer carry out its duties as Mandatory after 15 May 1948, and placed the fate of Palestine in the hands of the United Nations. The General Assembly of the United Nations voted on 29 November 1947 to partition the country between Arabs and Jews. Because of its unique religious character, the city of Jerusalem was to be under international control.

No sooner had the partition resolution been proclaimed than Zionist settlers started a terror campaign against Arab cities and villages. Jewish military strength, developed during the thirty years of Mandate, soon became evident. The Zionist campaign was not restricted to territory allotted to the Jewish state in the partition resolution, but penetrated deep into the Arab side as well. The Palestinian Arabs tried to resist, but were handicapped by lack of training and adequate weapons. A number of massacres, notably the one at the village of Deir Yassin on the night of 9/10 April 1948, caused many Arabs to flee for safety. During this surprise attack on a peaceful Arab village, 254 men, women and children were murdered and many of their bodies thrown down a well. Hundreds of thousands of Palestine's Arabs were rendered refugees. The neighbouring Arab countries rallied to support the Palestinians with arms and volunteers, but were unable to halt the aggression.

In the circumstances, the Arab states decided to use their regular armies in order to rescue the Arabs of Palestine. Accordingly the Arab Legion entered the Holy Land where it bore the brunt of the fighting. After protracted and bloody battles, it managed to save the Old City of Jerusalem and retain most of the territory allotted to the Arabs in the partition resolution.

The end of that round of fighting saw considerable gains for the Zionists who had augmented the territory of the newly declared State of Israel.

In December 1949, more than 2000 Palestinian notables and personalities met in Jericho and decided to ask King Abdullah to unite Palestine and Jordan formally under his crown. The Jordanian government agreed and on 11 April 1950 general elections were held on both banks of the river Jordan. On 24 April the newly elected Parliament ratified the union, and half a million Palestinian Arabs became Jordanian citizens, able to contribute fully to the life of the Hashemite Kingdom. The Palestinian part of the country became known as the West Bank, the old Transjordan as the East Bank.

King Abdullah and
Crown Prince Talal
in 1948

Now fate intervened with a cruel blow. On 20 July 1951, Abdullah Ibn Al Hussein, the realistic and courageous founder of the Kingdom of Jordan, was assassinated at the entrance to the Al Aqsa Mosque. Prince Talal, his eldest son, acceded to the throne but, owing to ill health, his reign lasted only a year. On 11 August 1952 Parliament decided to relieve King Talal of his duties and proclaim his eldest son, Crown Prince Hussein, constitutional monarch.

Since then Jordanians have associated the rapid progress and development of their country with the efforts exerted by 'Al Hussein', for the King's character is such that he confounds conventional notions about hereditary rulers and far surpasses the generally accepted standards of leadership. He is, in fact, by virtue of his background and training, ideally suited to tackle and solve the many problems facing Jordan and the Arab nation.

Hussein, son of Talal, son of Abdullah, son of Hussein, the Sharif of Mecca, was born in Amman on 14 November 1935. After attending a state school in Amman he then went to Alexandria and completed his secondary education at Victoria College. From there he travelled to England and attended Harrow and later, for his military training, The Royal Military Academy at Sandhurst, and The Royal Air Force College, Cranwell. He was eighteen when he assumed his constitutional duties.

At the time of his accession to the throne, Jordan was facing a series of Israeli raids on villages bordering the Armistice Line. One of these raids, on the village of Qibyah, on 14 October 1953, resulted in the destruction of forty-two houses and the death of fifty-three persons, mostly women and children. A national guard was recruited, but it was not able to protect the 600-kilometre Armistice Line.

44

Prince Hussein is proclaimed King of the Hashemite Kingdom of Jordan, 11 August 1952

Meanwhile, developments on the international level continued. The country's status was augmented when Jordan was accepted, on 14 December 1955, into membership of the United Nations.

Earlier that year, Great Britain, Turkey and Iraq invited Jordan to subscribe to the 'Baghdad Pact' which the three powers were contemplating. In spite of the fact that joining the pact would give Jordan additional strength and security, the idea was dropped, in deference to the strong objections of the other Arab states.

In those heady years the Arab countries were asserting their independence from the old imperial masters. Any special connection with a foreign power was increasingly looked down upon. Therefore, on 1 March 1956, King Hussein took a bold step when he relieved General Glubb, the Army Chief of Staff, and two other senior British officers of their duties. An Arab officer assumed command of the army and it was not long before the armed forces were staffed completely by Jordanian officers. The Anglo–Jordanian Treaty of 1946, which the King felt conflicted with Jordan's national sovereignty, was terminated on 13 March 1957 and the last British soldier left Jordan in July that year. After a brief period of adjustment, relations between the two countries developed along new lines of understanding and equality.

The first half of 1957 witnessed considerable unrest. Several political parties, in their struggle for power, tried to influence national policy by extraparliamentary means. Some Arab states also failed to live up to their pledge of subsidizing the budget in lieu of Great Britain. The young King took charge of a chaotic situation. A new cabinet was formed which dissolved the political parties and within a short period law and order were restored to the country.

Shortly thereafter, on 14 February 1958, the Arab Federation, uniting Jordan and Iraq, was proclaimed. A Federal Cabinet and Parliament were formed, but hopes for a promising future were shattered by the *coup d'état* of 14 July 1958 which brought the monarchy in Iraq to an end. Many members of the Hashemite family, including King Feisal II, Hussein's cousin, were assassinated.

A period of political estrangement followed, during which Jordan stood its ground under the leadership of King Hussein. Relations with Iraq were resumed in 1960, and Jordan participated in the two Arab summit conferences of 1964.

By now the country was making steady progress in many fields—in the economy, industry, education and communications. Factories were established, dams built, lands irrigated, more trees planted, the Bedouin of the desert settled, and tourism promoted. Tension eased with these domestic advances, and as political differences with Jordan's Arab neighbours came to an end, there was new hope for the future. Constitutional continuity was ensured when Prince Hassan, the King's younger brother, was proclaimed Crown Prince on 1 April 1965.

Such was Jordan's situation when danger suddenly loomed in April 1967. Five months earlier, the Israelis had attacked the Jordanian village of Samou' and inflicted heavy damage and losses, but no one thought then that that raid was a prelude to total war.

The chain of events which led to the conflict was started by an Israeli attack on Syrian bases on 7 April 1967. Egypt took certain steps in support of Syria, among them the closing of the Straits of Tiran. Jordan could not remain aloof in a dangerous situation affecting the Arab states in general and those bordering Israel in particular. Israeli mobilization prompted King Hussein to conclude a mutual defence agreement with Egypt on 30 May. A few days later, on 5 June 1967, Israel launched surprise attacks on airfields in Egypt, Syria, Jordan and Iraq. With the destruction of the Egyptian Air Force on the ground, the war was lost by the Arabs. The Jordanian army engaged the enemy in several battles, but owing to lack of air cover it was forced to retreat.

Despite United Nations cease-fire orders, Israeli forces continued the offensive and in subsequent days occupied the West Bank of Jordan, Sinai, Sharm As Sheikh and the Golan Heights. On 29 June Israel annexed the Holy City of Jerusalem, an action declared illegal by the UN General Assembly which called upon the Zionist state to rescind.

In a vigorous diplomatic effort to present the Arab viewpoint, King Hussein embarked on a campaign during the second half of 1967 which included visits to eight Middle Eastern and North African countries, attendance of an Arab conference at Khartoum, visits to Turkey, Iran and, for the first time, the Soviet Union. He also went to Algeria and several Western capitals, including Washington, and New York, where he participated in UN General Assembly debates on the Middle East.

The Security Council, on 22 November 1967, adopted a resolution calling for the establishment of just and lasting peace in the Middle East. It stipulated the withdrawal of Israeli troops from the territories occupied in the June war and the recognition of the sovereignty, territorial integrity and political independence of all states in the area. Egypt, Jordan and Syria eventually accepted the resolution, but the Israelis have thwarted every attempt to reach a final settlement.

As a result of the war, a Palestinian resistance movement developed within Israel proper, inside the occupied territories and abroad. The Israelis retaliated by launching damaging raids against Jordan, resulting in heavy losses in lives

King Hussein with world leaders. *Left to right in descending order:*

His Holiness Pope Paul VI; President Jimmy Carter of the United States; Her Majesty Queen Elizabeth II of Great Britain
President Giscard d'Estaing at the Elysée; President Nicolae Ceausescu of Romania

Emperor Hirohito of Japan; Iraqi President Saddam Hussain; King Khaled of Saudi Arabia

Sheikh Zayed bin Sultan Al Nahyan, President of United Arab Emirates; the late Sheikh Abdullah Al Salim Al Sabah of Kuwait; President Hafez Al Assad of Syria

and property. In its continuing campaign of destruction in the Jordan Valley, Israel launched a major attack across the Jordan River on the village of Karameh on 21 March 1968. In a fierce battle, the Jordanian army forced the invaders to withdraw after inflicting heavy casualties on them. Israel was censured by the UN Security Council, but its raids against Jordanian villages continued, driving the inhabitants out of the valley and thus paralysing the economy.

In spite of internal and external pressures Jordan was able, through its policy of moderation, to win the confidence and respect of the Arab countries. Relations with Saudi Arabia had been close since 1957, and co-operation with Egypt and Syria improved remarkably as a result of Jordan's active participation in the October war of 1973. In 1975, King Hussein and Syrian President Hafez Al Assad exchanged visits and a Jordanian-Syrian High Commission was formed to co-ordinate economic, social and foreign policy activities. Since then major economic and trade agreements between the two countries have been announced and joint ventures implemented.

King Hussein's effectiveness springs from the fact that while he is a most progressive monarch, he does not for a moment forget the rich Islamic tradition to which he is heir. His sense of history, his awareness of his Hashemite heritage, has enabled him to play a vital role as spokesman for the Arab world. For all his sophistication, he remains thoroughly of the country, and maintains intimate contact with his people and the ministries of his government. Audiences are held daily in an uninterrupted session that may last anywhere from three to six hours and include up to thirty different people from different walks of life. The people refer to him as 'Our Hussein', demonstrating a relationship of trust between the citizen and his chosen leader rare among nations. Hussein learned much during his boyhood from his grandfather, who was his constant mentor and affectionate companion. One of his first lessons, often repeated and never forgotten, was, 'Believe in God and serve the people'.

In his autobiography, *Uneasy Lies the Head,* King Hussein writes of the philosophy he has evolved in order to cope with a life of continuous strain, both in the pressures of administration and in the rigours of resisting the numerous attacks on his country:

The philosophy embraces a firm concept of Arab unity, tolerance, love of God, love of good deeds, [and] a deep rooted sense of justice.

This creed became a part of the young King's life on that fateful day in 1951, when he was a witness to the assassination of his beloved grandfather. As the two were about to enter the Aqsa Mosque, a man stepped out from behind a door and shot the venerable Abdullah at point-blank range. Another shot, also fired at close range, hit a medal on Hussein's chest and ricocheted.

On that terrible day, . . . I learned the importance of death; that when you have to die, you die, for it is God's judgement. Only thus have I found [the] particular inner peace granted to those who do not fear death.

He came to the throne, in 1952, of a country with few natural resources, the development of which had only just begun; a country, furthermore, whose

population had recently been swelled by more than a half a million people driven from their homes in Palestine. The 1948 hostilities had also severely affected the country's economic resources.

Nothing daunted, Jordan, under the guidance of her energetic young sovereign, embarked upon a programme of development the results of which have been outstanding. By dint of hard work, planning, and a spirit of determination, the Hashemite Kingdom today is a modern country, where free people are resolved to make their national life a model of progress for the entire Middle East. Jordan is not yet what it wishes to be–economically self-supporting–but advances are being made towards that goal.

The standard of education is high–probably the highest in the Arab world. Schools, health services and roads are all being improved and large and small industrial projects are springing up throughout the country.

As the King approached the twenty-fifth year of his reign, he inaugurated a Five-Year Plan of economic and social development, covering every aspect of the national life and the people's aspirations. Addressing an international conference which met in Amman in May 1976 to launch the $2·3 billion plan, the King called it:

. . . not merely a programme of action for the next five years, but a living example and shining model of serious partnership in thought, word and deed. It is, in all certainty, a major step that we take together along the path of building a future which will provide its generations with opportunities that our own generations have sorely missed.

The quality of King Hussein's leadership has been proved over and again during his twenty-five year reign. He is a man of deep humanity, perhaps unique among the world's rulers in the number of amnesties he has granted individuals under sentence for various kinds of offence. Many of those pardoned and given another chance have attained high positions in the service of the state.

His compassion and modesty lead him to treat Jordanians as brothers rather than as subjects. In times of distress he is the first to come forward with help. His countrymen are his family, for whose welfare he works tirelessly and with unbounded dedication. For these and many other qualities, he has gained the loyalty, love and respect of all.

5 The Land, its People, its Cities

Jordan is one of the smaller countries on the eastern borders of the Mediterranean, that ancient zone of settlement and transit where civilization had its beginnings. Situated south of Syria, between latitudes 29° and 33° North and longitudes 34° and 39° East, the territory stretches from Lake Tiberias and the Yarmouk River in the north to the Gulf of Aqaba in the south, where it borders the north-western corner of the Arabian Peninsula. Eastwards the boundaries are not defined by any geographical features, but merge into the deserts of Iraq and Saudi Arabia. The total area, including the Dead Sea, is 96 188 square kilometres. On the west, the country straddles the Jordan River and the Dead Sea, but by far the greater part of the territory, all but 6·3 per cent, is on the East Bank. Jordan is not quite landlocked; it has a 40-kilometre coral-bordered stretch of coast on the Red Sea at Aqaba.

More than four-fifths of Jordan is desert or semi-desert, but to say that is to give a wrong impression of the Kingdom's variety and fascination. It is a country of contrasts. The east is a vast desert plateau, the west a mountainous region, consisting of two tablelands rising to a height of 600 to 1000 metres. Between the two mountain areas lies one of the strangest landscapes in the world, a north-to-south rift valley from 200 to 400 metres below sea level. It is the deepest depression on the face of the earth.

Through that valley flows the river Jordan. In it also lies the Dead Sea, a body of water with the unique characteristic that, owing to its mineral density, even heavy objects do not sink in it. The valley contains the richest agricultural land in the country, watered by tributaries of the Jordan River and producing sub-tropical fruit and vegetables for export as well as home consumption.

Elsewhere, the land is very dry, with a few green oases in the wilderness of scrub and sand. Rainfall is slight everywhere, averaging 400 millimetres in the highlands, 200 in the rift valley and less than 50 in the desert. The distribution of vegetation follows the pattern of rainfall: pine and oak forests where rainfall is heaviest; grass and shrubs in the semi-arid steppes; thorn and sparse shrubs where there is least rain.

The prevailing westerly winds draw that moisture from the Mediterranean and deposit it over the highlands of north-eastern Jordan. Winds reaching southern Jordan blow across north Africa and carry little moisture. Consequently the south-eastern heights receive less rain than those of the north. The occasional eastern winds from central Asia are hot and dusty in summer, cold and dry in winter.

Hill country in
northern Jordan

In this Mediterranean climate the winters, from October to the end of April, are mild; indeed it is more correct to speak of the rainy season than the winter.

The summer season, between June and October, is warm and sunny, the evenings refreshingly cool. In the desert there is a more severe contrast between day and night, when the temperature sometimes drops to below zero. The highlands have an average maximum temperature of 33°C in summer, and rarely less than 7°C in winter. In the Jordan Valley the temperature reaches 40°C in summer and seldom falls below 14°C in winter.

The temperature on the whole is gentle, but the terrain is in many respects harsh. This harshness provides interest and adventure for the tourist, but problems and challenges for the Jordanians. They are winning produce from the small patches of cultivable soil, phosphates and other minerals from the barren lands. In the mountains and plateaux they are prospecting for what is believed to be considerable unexploited mineral wealth. So far no oil has been discovered under the sands of Jordan, but it is abundant in neighbouring Arab countries, and exploration continues hopefully.

This varied geography has bred a versatile and energetic people. The population, little more than two and a half million, reveals a variety of cultures, and reflects the legacy of the centuries. The Bedouin roaming the desert with their flocks of

The shores of the Dead Sea, lowest point on earth
Above left: Gorge of the river Mujib shortly before it reaches the Dead Sea

52

Floods in the desert after
sudden rain

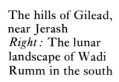

The hills of Gilead,
near Jerash
Right: The lunar
landscape of Wadi
Rumm in the south

Far left: Red anemones carpet the fields in spring

Date palm in the Jordan Valley

Flower of an Indian fig tree

sheep and goats live and practise their traditional arts and crafts very much as their ancestors did in biblical times. They are a small but highly distinctive section of the population.

The majority of Jordanians are engaged in cultivation, mining and trade, and are becoming more and more industrialized and urbanized. They are concentrated largely in the north-western strip of the country, running due north and south, taking in the valley of the Jordan River and the territories served by the two great highways leading down to the Red Sea and the southern frontier with Saudi Arabia.

Many of Jordan's modern cities are built on layer upon layer of ancient towns, so that on the same site there is evidence of centuries of human occupation.

The heritage of the centuries is manifested in the life-style of the people as well as in the buildings. Old-world alleyways and *souks* (markets) are only a short walk from shopping centres and office buildings as up-to-date as any in the world.

The capital, Amman, is believed to be one of the oldest continuously inhabited cities in the world. Since Amir Abdullah made it his capital after the first World War, Amman has grown from an insignificant town of some 6000 inhabitants into a bustling metropolis of 750 000. Originally built, like Rome, on seven hills, it has spread in recent years over another five as well as a large area of the surrounding countryside.

The modern city is the seat of the national government. From its streets radiate the country's major highways. It is the Kingdom's business and financial centre, with Jordanian and foreign banks, the headquarters of industrial organizations and a growing number of industrial plants, including the very new addition of a steel-rolling mill. Amman has a Chamber of Commerce, as indeed have many of the other cities, and a Chamber of Industry. It has an international

Bedouin from central
Jordan
Top: Fruit seller in
Jerusalem

airport, rail communication with Aqaba in the south and Syria in the north, road connection with the neighbouring countries and daily flights to dozens of the world's major capitals. A cluster of royal palaces—including the Raghadan, built by Amir Abdullah, and the Basman, which houses the Royal Hashemite Court—dominates one of the original seven hills.

In addition to elementary, preparatory and secondary schools for boys and girls, numerous vocational training centres and other institutions of specialized education, Amman houses one of the Kingdom's two universities—the University of Jordan—which boasts one of the finest medical centres in the Middle East. The capital's schools, where English or French are invariably taught as a second language, are the best in the country.

Amman is also the centre from which tours depart to all the historical sites and beauty spots in the country. Its excellent hotels make it the obvious base for the growing influx of tourists. It is a natural centre for the exploration of the Jordan Valley and, in its own right, a recreational centre, with night clubs, cinemas, theatres, race courses, ice-skating rinks and facilities for other sports.

One of the most impressive recent developments is the Hussein Youth City, a modern complex of buildings enclosing a main stadium seating approximately 25 000 spectators, used for football, track and field events and various kinds of spectacles and festivals; two other football and track fields used for minor competitions; a swimming area containing three pools, all constructed according to Olympic standards; tennis courts and sections for badminton, volley ball and basketball; a separate clubhouse complex consisting of a gymnasium, four squash courts, a recreation hall, a cafeteria and a conference hall. The Palace of Culture, its handsome architectural design reminiscent of a winged Bedouin tent, is visible from the main road.

Next to Amman in population and commercial importance are Zarqa, with 300 000 inhabitants, and Irbid, with 116 000. Zarqa is a fast-growing, entirely new town—a symbol of Jordan's industrial future. There is an oil refinery and a tannery on the outskirts.

Irbid is one of the 'ancient and modern' cities, built on a mound under which lie several Irbids of past centuries. Relics of the past remain, notably part of the basalt wall that surrounded the town and a vast Crusader fortress from which the Frankish garrison conducted secret correspondence by carrier pigeon. Irbid is surrounded by rich agricultural land, which, no doubt, was the reason for its settlement in early times and its prominence as one of the member cities of the Decapolis. Today, its people work in industry and agriculture; it is one of the Kingdom's granaries. It is also the seat of a Governorate and of the Yarmouk University, the Kingdom's second institution of higher education.

Karak, south of Amman on the King's Highway, is a busy prosperous little town. A former Moabite capital, important also in Byzantine times, it is still noted for its citadel, built by the Crusaders. Like Irbid and Salt it is the centre of a wide fertile area.

Salt, with a population of about 20 000, engaged mainly in agriculture, has always been an outlet for the food production of the Jordan Valley. It is the seat of a Governorate and an attractive summer resort.

One of the fastest growing Jordanian cities, both in population and in prosperity, is Aqaba. Located at the head of the Gulf of Aqaba, it provided a rare natural

Ramadan prayers at the
Al Hussein Mosque,
Amman
Left: Residential
suburb of Amman

Al Hussein Youth City
–ultra-modern sport
and leisure centre

The commercial port of Aqaba on the Red Sea

harbour in ancient times. Today, it still enjoys its position as the only outlet to the sea for a large inland region. The city's earliest mention dates from the tenth century BC when it was recommended for its sweet water. Like so many Jordanian towns it was a centre for Crusader activity, but then fell into decline for centuries, to awaken to a new and vigorous life at the turn of the twentieth century.

Before the First World War Aqaba was a humble fishing village. With the founding of the Hashemite Kingdom, it was seen as a potential gateway to the commercial world. Even so, it had no more than 1700 inhabitants at the time of the Second World War. In the thirty years or so since then its population has multiplied tenfold and it has developed into a port with worldwide trade. The harbour is crowded with shipping and from it go out the phosphates mined at Hasa and other Jordanian exports.

Aqaba is still a fishing port. It has a Marine Science Station and is the base of the Jordanian Federation of Underwater Activities. It has the nation's second airport, and is linked by rail to Amman, and beyond it to the Syrian border. Miles of sandy beach at Aqaba, shelving gently into safe sea water, have procured for the town a growing reputation as a seaside playground.

The chief cities of the West Bank, too, are modern as well as ancient, with industry, commerce and tourism jostling the historic and sacred places. Jerusalem is an occupied city but the portion inside the ancient city wall (and in recent years spilling beyond them) has a population of about 70 000 Arabs. Its modern hotels accommodate thousands of visitors and pilgrims every year.

Bethlehem is a charming town with olive groves and green terraces, famous of course as a place of pilgrimage. It has a flourishing needlework industry and produces *objets d'art* in mother of pearl.

Nablus, the ancient city of Shekim, has a population of 60 000, and a number of industries, producing olive oil, soap and vegetable ghee.

Hebron is another historic city which is more than a museum piece. It is a major agricultural centre, famous for its fig plantations and vineyards. It is also a beautiful summer resort. And Ramallah, set in a leafy area over 700 metres above sea level, is a tourist centre with fine hotels and restaurants.

6 Constitution and Government

The Constitution of the Hashemite Kingdom of Jordan was promulgated on 8 January 1952 and has since been amended to meet the changing requirements of the Kingdom. Executive authority resides in the Monarch. The Monarchy is hereditary, the crown being passed by the King to his eldest son, although the King may, at his discretion, nominate one of his brothers as Heir Apparent. The Constitution stipulates that the Monarch should be a direct descendant of King Abdullah Ibn Hussein, founder of the Kingdom.

Prince Hassan, the younger of King Hussein's two brothers, was proclaimed Crown Prince of the Hashemite Kingdom of Jordan on 1 April 1965.

The King attains his majority at the age of eighteen, calculated according to the Lunar Calendar. If the Heir Apparent accedes to the throne before he is eighteen, a Regent or a Regency Council exercises power on his behalf until he comes of age. If the King is incapacitated or is absent from the Kingdom, he appoints a Regent or a Regency Council to exercise power as prescribed in the Royal Decree of Appointment. If the King is absent for more than four months, Parliament must be convened to consider the situation.

Upon accession to the throne, the King takes the constitutional oath before Parliament. As Head of State, he is immune from all liability and responsibility. He receives foreign envoys, confers honours and medals for meritorious service, grants special pardons and remits sentences. Money is printed or minted in his name. On the recommendation of the Cabinet, or sometimes of the Prime Minister, he appoints all senior government civil servants and high officials.

The King ratifies and issues laws and regulations. He is the Supreme Commander of the armed land, sea and air forces; he declares war, concludes peace and signs treaties. He appoints the President and members of the Senate (the Upper House of Parliament) and accepts their resignations. He orders the holding of elections for the House of Representatives (the Lower House of Parliament) and inaugurates, adjourns, prorogues and dissolves the House.

The King appoints the Prime Minister, and other ministers upon the recommendation of the Prime Minister.

The Parliament of Jordan is the National Assembly, composed of the Senate and the House of Representatives. The supreme legislative authority in the Kingdom is vested in 'The King-in-the-National-Assembly'; that is, the King and the two Houses. The Senate is composed of thirty members appointed by the King for meritorious service or other special qualifications. The minimum age for Senate membership is forty years. The House of Representatives is composed of sixty deputies, freely elected by adult male and female suffrage. They are

elected either in a general election, which takes place after a House has been dissolved, or in a by-election when a vacancy occurs in the House. The minimum age for membership of the House is thirty years. The House of Representatives alone is empowered to pass a vote of confidence or no confidence in a Government.

The chief officer of the Senate is the President, who is appointed by the King. The chief officer of the House of Representatives is the Speaker (President of the House of Representatives) who is elected by the deputies at the beginning of each new session.

The term of each House is four years. The term of the House of Representatives can be prolonged one year or more at the King's discretion. During each year of their Parliamentary term, the two Houses hold one ordinary session of four months, and as many extraordinary sessions as may be necessary when invited to do so by Royal Decree.

At the beginning of each ordinary session, each House elects two standing committees and as many other committees as it deems necessary for the discharge of its duties. The standing committees are the financial and the judicial, and the other committees usually include foreign affairs, education, agriculture, refugees, tourism, and public guidance. Each committee elects its own chairman and *rapporteur,* and holds as many meetings as the situation requires.

A Bill is initiated in the House of Representatives. If there is no urgent reason for its immediate discussion, it is referred to the appropriate committee for study and report. After passing through the committee stage, the Bill is presented to the House for debate and voting. After the approval of the House, the Speaker forwards the Bill to the Senate, where it passes through the same process as in the lower House. When approved by both Houses, the Bill is submitted to the King who gives consent in a Royal Decree. The King may return the Bill unapproved in which case it is debated once again by both Houses. Should the two Houses pass the Bill a second time by a two-thirds majority, it becomes an Act of Parliament.

A Bill also becomes an Act of Parliament if it is neither returned to Parliament nor approved by Royal Decree within a period of six months. Disagreement between the two Houses on any provisions in the Bill is decided by two-thirds majority vote in a joint session of both Houses.

The members of either House may initiate Bills, ask questions and demand a general debate on any subject if a minister's reply is deemed unsatisfactory.

No member of either House may be detained or tried during its session, except with the express approval of the House to which he belongs. In the event of a member's arrest while committing a crime, the House to which he belongs must be notified immediately. Each member of the Senate or of the House of Representatives enjoys complete freedom of speech and of expression within the bounds of the Constitution and the Rules of Order of his House. No legal proceedings can be taken against any member because of any vote or opinion expressed or speech made during debates. No member can be impeached except by a vote of a two-thirds majority of his House.

King Hussein opening the third ordinary session of the ninth Jordanian Parliament

Judges are appointed by Royal Decree in accordance with the provisions of the law. They are independent of both the Legislature and the Executive, and exercise their powers as defined by law.

The Courts, including the Supreme Court of Appeal, are divided into three categories: Civil Courts, Religious Courts and Special Courts. The Civil Courts include Courts of First Instance, Magistrates' Courts, Courts of Cassation, and Courts of Appeal, and deal with civil and criminal cases. They are open to, and have jurisdiction over, all persons in the Kingdom, including the Government. There is no need to seek permission before involving the Government.

The High Court of Justice is also one of the Civil Courts. This is the only Court in Jordan which deals with administrative law. It has powers to examine and rescind ministerial and other administrative decisions.

The Religious Courts include the Muslim Shari'a Courts, which deal with all matters of personal law for Muslims, and the Religious Community Councils, which deal with similar matters for non-Muslims.

The Special Courts are formed in accordance with the provisions of the law, for the trial of certain cases. They are mainly the Military Court and the State Security Court.

A principal feature of the legal system of Jordan is the distinction made between criminal and civil law. The criminal law is concerned with wrongs against the community as a whole; criminal proceedings are initiated and conducted by the Attorney General or Public Prosecutors. The civil law is concerned with the rights and obligations of individual members of the community and proceedings are instituted by the aggrieved person. Civil cases are frequently settled privately before or during the actual hearing. The jury system is not used in Jordan, and actions are tried, according to the seriousness of the case, by one judge as in the Magistrates' Court, by two or three judges as in the Court of Cassation, or by five judges as in the Supreme Court of Appeal.

The Prime Minister, nominated by the King, forms the Cabinet, and he and the ministers take oath before the King upon assuming office. The Cabinet should submit a statement of its programme for the approval of the House of Representatives within one month of its formation. If the House is dissolved or is not in session, the Speech from the Throne can be considered a statement of the Cabinet programme.

Neither the Prime Minister nor the ministers need to be members of either House of Parliament. If any of them is a member, he does not draw the emoluments of his membership. Whether they are members or not they have the right to address both Houses of Parliament. If they are members they can vote like other members.

The Prime Minister and the ministers are collectively responsible to the House of Representatives for the initiation and direction of national policy. They are each responsible for the conduct of their own respective ministries and departments. They must attend sessions of the two Houses of Parliament to answer questions and defend and seek approval for Government policy and legislation.

A vote of confidence in the Cabinet or in any minister can be taken by the House of Representatives at the request of the Prime Minister or any ten or more members of the House. Failure to obtain the vote of confidence by absolute majority entails the resignation of the Cabinet or the minister as the case may be. The King's orders, written or oral, do not absolve the ministers from liability.

King Hussein, and on his right Crown Prince Hassan, take the salute in front of Parliament House for the opening of the fifth session of the ninth Jordanian National Assembly

Ministers can be tried for crimes committed in the performance of their ministerial duties before a Parliamentary High Council composed of the President of the Senate, three members of the Senate and the five judges of the Supreme Court of Appeal. During trial, the minister is suspended from office.

The Cabinet meets regularly twice or three times a week, and is sometimes presided over by the King in his capacity as Head of State. The Prime Minister and the ministers sign the resolutions of the Cabinet and submit them to the King for ratification in certain cases as prescribed by law. The proceedings and resolutions of the Cabinet are strictly confidential, except where they are authorized by the Prime Minister to be disclosed or to be made public in official communiqués.

The Cabinet is the supreme executive body which presides over and controls Government. It does so through ministers, vice-presidents of statutory bodies attached to the Prime Minister and local government councils. The Cabinet has power to form, from time to time as the need arises, departmental committees and public or semi-public commissions, to undertake specific inquiries or studies and make recommendations. Committees and commissions are granted inter-ministerial and inter-departmental powers, to enable them to carry out their duties.

The Prime Minister's Office is the meeting place of the Cabinet. It has a permanent secretary and staff of civil servants and advisors. Attached to this office are statutory bodies, including the Executive Office for the Affairs of the Occupied Territories, which became later a ministerial office, and the Natural Resources

Authority. A number of independent departments report to the Prime Minister's Office and so, of course, do all the Government ministers.

King Hussein presiding over a Cabinet meeting at the Prime Minister's Office

The main pattern of local government organization is the division of the country into the Governorates of Amman, Balqa'a, Irbid, Karak, Ma'an, Jerusalem, Hebron and Nablus. Each Governorate is headed by a Governor, and is sub-divided into administrative regions. It is advised by an appointed Advisory Committee of the local heads of departments and representatives of Municipalities, Chambers of Commerce, public organizations and members selected on the grounds of their experience or specialist knowledge. The Governors enjoy wide administrative authority, and exercise, in certain specific matters, the powers of ministers. The purpose is to eliminate red tape, facilitate administration, and provide better public services at the local level, as well as to supervise the collection of taxes, and to attend to the general affairs of the Governorate. The only exception is the administration of justice.

The boards of town and village councils are all elected by the free vote of resident adults. The mayors and presidents of rural councils are appointed by the Council of Ministers from among the members, but deputy-mayors and vice-presidents are elected by their own boards. Municipal and rural councils enjoy wide autonomy in the administration of local public services, including water distribution, town planning, the maintenance of roads within their boundaries and the provision of some social assistance and service to needy persons.

The democratic system of government in Jordan is further augmented and reinforced by diverse organizations and associations voluntarily formed and administered by various categories of people, with the purpose of preserving and promoting the interests of their respective professions, vocations, business activities, cultural aptitudes or philanthropic services.

These organizations cover a wide field of activities, and their elected boards address the Government on subjects pertaining to their respective activities. They can criticize orders, regulations and Bills which touch on their activities. They act as voluntary advisors to the Government and to Parliament. They may press for their demands to be met or complain of any measures which in their opinion adversely affect public welfare and interests. They are governed by legislation, which can be modified or amended on their own initiative.

The Constitution of the Hashemite Kingdom of Jordan incorporates a Bill of Rights guaranteeing the personal equality of all Jordanians and their right to equal opportunities, security from illegal detention, freedom of movement and residence within the Kingdom, sanctity of personal property, freedom of worship, freedom of opinion and association (including freedom of expression in the press and publications), the right of assembly and freedom to form societies and trade unions. The Constitution also gives the individual freedom of access to all public authorities. It specifies that the State must provide an education for every Jordanian within its abilities. Elementary and preparatory education (a total of nine years) is obligatory and free for Jordanians in all Government schools, and the Government supervises the curriculum in all private schools. All Jordanians have the right to assume public office.

Work is a right for all Jordanians, and the State guarantees work for all Jordanians within its capacity. The State protects labour by legislation. Wages, hours of work and paid holidays and annual leave are regulated by law. The law guarantees the payment of special compensation to workers supporting families, and also termination benefits, old age and sickness benefits and workers' compensation. The employment of women and minors is regulated. Workshops and factories are required to observe safety regulations. The Constitution further provides for prohibition of compulsory labour except in certain public emergencies or by a judicial decision.

Political refugees are guaranteed protection if they take refuge within the Kingdom on account of their political beliefs. The extradition of ordinary criminals is regulated by treaty.

7 The Armed Forces

One of Jordan's most triumphant achievements in the march towards independence has been the development of an effective army and air force. The Jordanian armed forces have their origin in the army of the Great Arab Revolt which set out from Mecca in 1916 under the command of Sharif Hussein Ibn Ali. They have inherited the mission of the Revolt—to achieve unity, freedom and a better life for the Arab nation.

The nucleus of the famous Arab Legion was formed from a small number of soldiers who took part in the Arab Revolt. They were then about 250 irregular fighters, who accompanied Amir Abdullah when he arrived in Jordan in the early 1920s.

Amir Abdullah's first task on arrival in Transjordan was to secure the independence of this portion of the Arab homeland and to quell inter-tribal feuding. The circumstances were extremely difficult. The conspiracies which had come to light after the First World War and the dangers threatening Syria prompted him to contemplate the formation of a strong standing army to protect the newly formed state. These forces would later be used to obtain independence from the British.

Jordan's army began with one company of cavalry, one company of infantry, a machine-gun unit, a signals section and a band. Until 1923, the total number did not exceed 750 men. Under its first commander, Colonel F.G. Peake, whose Arab officers had been trained in the old Ottoman army, the Arab Legion became a mould and a melting pot, an instrument for social reform as well as national security.

The Legion continued to grow until its numbers reached about 1100 in 1930. In 1931, the first Desert Patrol was founded to maintain law and order. Commanded by a Captain John Bagot Glubb, it was recruited mainly from the Bedouin themselves. The first mechanized force was formed in 1933 with only three vehicles; their numbers, including a camel corps, amounted to about 120. This force took over the task of maintaining security and preventing inter-tribal raids, especially from without the country.

With the outbreak of the Second World War the Arab Legion, now under the command of General Glubb, known in Jordan as 'Glubb Pasha', had reached a strength of 1600 men. It saw active and honourable service against the forces of fascism in Iraq and Syria. Amir Abdullah, however, took advantage of Britain's preoccupation on other fronts to reinforce and organize his armed forces on new lines. Individual flag troops were formed, and the first regular regiment was constituted and later named the First Brigade. In 1942, the second regiment was

Behind the Commander-in-Chief, jet fighters of the Royal Jordanian Airforce

67

Amir Abdullah in 1941 inspecting the mechanized units of the Arab Legion. These are machine-gun carrying armoured Rolls-Royce cars

formed, and this became the Second Brigade. In the wake of the war, the Arab Legion continued to expand both in numbers and equipment until in 1948 it had three brigades, two garrison battalions and a fourth regiment.

The second stage in the development of the army spans 1948–67. By the end of the Second World War, the Middle East had experienced conditions which helped strengthen and organize the Arab Legion. The Legion had also benefited from combat techniques and methods used in the war, and learned from co-operation with the Allied armies the value and art of protecting lines of communication.

The British Mandate in Palestine had tried to give effect to the Zionist dream of setting up a national home for the Jews in the Holy Land, in accordance with the Balfour Declaration which pledged Britain's assistance. During and after the Second World War, numerous armed clashes took place between the Palestinian Arabs and the Jews, whose numbers had been swollen enormously by immigration. When in 1948 war broke out between the Arabs and the Israelis, the Jordanian armed forces played a heroic role in saving that substantial part of Palestine which remained under Arab control.

By the end of the first Arab–Israeli war in 1949, six infantry regiments had been formed. The Jordanian army thus consisted of an infantry division, an artillery brigade, a mortar battery, an artillery battery, an engineering and wireless regiment and a field aid regiment. By the end of 1967, however, a new armoured brigade had been established. The artillery brigade was also reorganized into three artillery field regiments and an anti-aircraft regiment.

Under the guidance of King Hussein the Jordanian armed forces grew in size and prestige. In March 1956, the young King, in his role of Commander-in-Chief

Artillery exercise with a 4·5 Howitzer field-piece
Top left: Motorized column of the Arab Legion. Land Rovers equipped for the desert with spare tanks of water and petrol
Right: Modified Centurion tanks dip their guns in salute on Army Day parade

of the armed forces, carried out his decision to Arabize the army and free it from its foreign command. Although respecting General Glubb personally, he realized that in the new political climate created by the rise of Israel it was imperative to give the army a new sense of responsibility and Arab pride. Accordingly he relieved Glubb and appointed Jordanians to all senior commands. The Arab Legion was renamed the Jordan Arab Army. The British soon ended their annual military subsidy, but King Hussein was able to replace it with aid from other Arab nations and from the United States.

This was a turning point in the history, command, organization and armament of the forces. King Hussein was now able to rebuild the army which his grand-father had formed, creating anew the army of the Great Arab Revolt—an army strong in will, capable of shouldering its national and pan-Arab responsibilities, and, in its development, coping with the most up-to-date military techniques.

In 1957, King Hussein ordered the formation of the Fourth Infantry Brigade and an additional Field Artillery Regiment. In 1958, heavy artillery was introduced. In the same year, the Armoured Brigade was reorganized to become the Armoured Army, and in 1961 it became the Armour Corps.

The 40th Brigade was formed within the First Fighting Groups; and in the Second Fighting Groups the 60th Armoured Brigade and the First Royal Guards Brigade came into being.

In 1965, the organization and development of the army made further progress when King Hussein ordered the formation of five infantry brigades, and the deployment of the army on two fronts: the Eastern and the Western. Ten infantry regiments were stationed on both fronts.

69

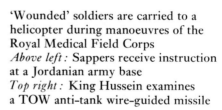

'Wounded' soldiers are carried to a
helicopter during manoeuvres of the
Royal Medical Field Corps
Above left: Sappers receive instruction
at a Jordanian army base
Top right: King Hussein examines
a TOW anti-tank wire-guided missile

March past of soldiers of the Jordan
Arab Army bearing regimental
colours

On 5 June 1967, the Kingdom of Jordan was forced to enter a war with Israel, the result of which was the loss of a precious part of the homeland. After the war, the armed forces underwent intensive overall reorganization. Within a remarkably short period of time, by introducing advanced weaponry and technological innovation, they were once again a formidable fighting force.

During this period, new types of artillery were introduced. M-60 tanks were procured, and rockets and up-to-date anti-tank weapons were also introduced. The infantry were equipped with the most modern individual weapon in the world, the M-16 rifle, as well as with guided missiles. Auxiliary arms and services, such as maintenance, communications, ordnance and medical services, were improved and expanded.

During the fourth Arab–Israeli war in 1973, King Hussein ordered the dispatch of a group of élite army brigades to the Syrian front, where they played an important part in repulsing the Israeli onslaught on Syrian territory.

The nucleus of the Royal Jordanian Air Force was formed on 22 July 1948 on the initiative of King Abdullah. This embryonic air force consisted of the propeller type of aircraft, used for training and for the transport of personnel and mail.

By the end of 1949 a group of young Jordanians had been sent abroad to train as pilots and maintenance officers. The first batch to qualify consisted of five transport pilots and three co-pilots.

When King Hussein assumed constitutional powers, he began to strengthen the air arm with jet fighters. He learned to fly every type of plane, from helicopters to jets, and personally tested every prospective purchase. Soon the air force was augmented by a number of Vampire fighter aircraft.

In 1959, a squadron of Hawker Hunter jet fighters and Whirlwind helicopters was brought in. In 1966, in the light of the development of air forces in the region, the Jordanian Air Force was supplied with the advanced F104 Starfighter.

In 1972, the air force was reorganized to keep pace with expansion. This included the construction of new air bases. Other types of aircraft were added, such as the American F5 fighter, the C119 and the C130. At the same time, a computer system was introduced to speed up and improve the services. The emphasis was now on continuous technical training in order to ensure an adequate reserve of efficient pilots trained to the highest modern standards.

In 1974 there were further advances in all spheres. These included improvement of training equipment, in order to end the need to send airmen abroad for training. At the end of 1975, the Directorate of Air Defence was created in order to improve Jordan's performance in combating enemy air strikes.

By strenuous effort, the King has made his armed forces the best organized and disciplined in the region, as both friend and enemy have testified. But there is another side to the development and deployment of the military which bears mention. Under the King, the armed forces have been encouraged to contribute towards the national life by making their skills and manpower available for social or civil projects. Not only does this help the economy in practical terms, it also strengthens the ties between those who serve and those whom they protect.

8 Culture and the Arts

In ancient times, Jordan was a melting pot for the cultures of many different peoples, both indigenous and invading. The present population of the area originates mainly in the Arabian Peninsula, in the outflow of Arab tribes heading northwards and becoming accepted by and assimilated with earlier civilizations.

With the advent of Islam in the seventh century, Islamic culture dominated the area, and gave it those characteristic features that have prevailed and matured for fourteen centuries. Since Islamic culture is so deeply rooted, it is difficult to speak of a separate Jordanian culture. The culture of Jordan is, in fact, an integral part of Arab culture.

Between the tenth and the seventeenth centuries many poets, writers, historians, geographers and commentators on religion and canon law had their origins in Jordan. However, intellectual life in the area deteriorated during the Ottoman period. It was revived late in the nineteenth century and in the first decades of the twentieth century. The period after the First World War saw the expansion of elementary and secondary education, the spread of foreign schools being accompanied by wider cultural relations with the neighbouring Arab countries. Many works were translated into Arabic from English, French, Russian, Italian and German. Newspapers and books became available and cultural clubs and societies were established.

One can understand, therefore, how the Jordanian state became a base for the liberty, the unity, and the struggle for a better life, of the Arabs as a whole. Its literature and its intellectual life generally reflect Arab ideals and national aspirations. From this historical cultural setting there emerges the concept of a Jordanian national culture, as the local manifestation of the wider Arab cultural complex.

Ceiling panel, from the Dome of the Rock

The years from 1921 to 1946, which constitute the Amirate era, saw a flowering of the romantic tradition in the country's literature. The late King Abdullah, himself a poet and a distinguished scholar, helped greatly to foster the literary movement in Jordan, especially poetry, which is traditionally the most advanced vehicle of Arab literary expression. Creative writing represented the national feelings and ideals of the rising Jordanian middle class. The movement on the East Bank soon caught up with a similar, though more advanced, movement in Palestine, then under the British Mandate.

After 1948 the two movements united and acquired an essentially Jordanian character. The most famous poet of the period was Mustafa Al Tal, a great Jordanian romantic, whose verse is still on the lips of his fellow countrymen. The years following 1948 witnessed the first seeds of realism in art and literature. The loss of a great part of Palestine and the influx of refugees into Jordan provided fertile soil for the development of realistic writing on the themes of social and political justice. Collections of poems and short stories began to appear in Amman and Jerusalem, and local literature flourished despite the harsh conditions in the publishing industry. In 1974 the Jordanian Writers' Society was established. It has more than 170 members. They include dramatists, novelists, short story writers, poets, literary critics and people engaged in research on folklore.

The early sixties saw the establishment of the theatrical movement. It was led by a Jordanian stage director who, with the help of an endowment, established the Jordanian Theatre Group. With government encouragement this group embarked enthusiastically on projects which took them outside the country to Syria, Iraq and other Arab lands. The University of Jordan embraced the movement and lent its technical facilities, and soon other drama groups were formed and flourished.

The Department of Culture and Arts, as part of the Ministry of Information and Culture, established its experimental threatre in adjacent premises with seating for 400 spectators. The government, however, decided that a vigorous theatre movement required a well-equipped theatre centre. In the early seventies the Youth Welfare Organization started work on the establishment of the Jordanian Royal Theatre. This is a complex of three theatres, the first with 400 seats, the second with 1000, and the third a 'mini-theatre' for rehearsals but also convertible into a circular cafeteria.

In 1976 the Ministry of Culture and Youth was formed to reorganize and foster the cultural activities initiated by the government. Its first act was to host the first Conference of Arab Ministers of Culture, the outcome of which was the 'Declaration of Amman', which voiced the Arab desire to create a unified culture throughout the Arab world. The ministry is preparing legislation aimed at giving practical expression to the movement.

One of these ordinances has led to the formation of the Jordanian Painters' Society. The society is establishing a permanent gallery for art exhibitions. Contemporary Jordanian painters and sculptors are well known in the Arab world, and some have exhibited in France, Spain, Britain, the USA, Italy, and the Soviet Union, as well as in other Asian countries.

The earliest known examples of representational painting in Jordan are the murals at Qasr Amra, probably completed by the Caliph Walid I around AD 715. These depict dancers, musicians, royalty, hunting scenes and other human and animal forms. Besides the scenes of everyday life, ornamental designs, derived from geometric and floral figures, or Arabic scripts, were included in the murals. There are also geometric decorations in the frieze of the Al Mushatta palace, which dates back to the eighth century. The frieze was presented to the German Kaiser just before the First World War and is still displayed at the East Berlin Museum.

In the nineteenth century David Roberts's pencil and watercolour sketches made the archaeological and Holy Places of Jordan well known all over the world.

The Royal Cultural
Centre
Right: Sculpture class
at the Institute of Fine
Arts

Eighth-century fresco
at Qasr Amra

The pioneers of modern painting in Jordan, however, were non-Jordanian. The first exhibition of contemporary Jordanian art was held at Muntada Al Arabi Club in Amman in the early 1950s. Those who participated were the amateurs who now form the nucleus of Jordan's professional painters.

Political instability, the war in 1948, Israeli aggression and the explusion of Palestinians from their homeland affected the modern movement and influenced Jordanian painters with themes of tragedy and disaster.

In 1953 the Jordan Art Association was formed, followed by the Sculpture Association in 1965. They have held many exhibitions and have played a major role in encouraging painters.

The growing appreciation of art induced some talented amateurs to study abroad at fine art academies. This quickening interest and the discovery of latent talent among Jordanians prompted the establishment in late 1971 of an Institute of Fine Arts within the Department of Culture and Arts.

Sculpture is taught at the Fine Arts Institute. Calligraphy, a traditional Muslim art form, is still practised by some contemporary artists. It has also influenced modern painting. The art of ceramics has always flourished in Arab and Islamic culture, and the present-day Jordanian ceramic artists carry on the tradition.

The music of Jordan is essentially folk music. Its present forms draw heavily on Bedouin and Islamic origins. They range from Arabic folk songs and religious melodies to contemporary compositions which combine local elements and Western classical style.

Bedouin tradition is evident in the *hijaini*, a singing style originally set to the rhythm of the camel's gait. Islamic origins are felt in the special type of folk music used in recitals of religious texts. All are chanted in traditional melody.

Jordanian folk music embraces most daily activities. There are songs for work, watering, marching, weddings, etc. These utilize the three-quarter tone, together

Interior of the Dome of
the Rock showing the
intricate mosaic work
and calligraphy
Above right: Detail of
the interior of the
Dome of the Rock.
Arch, tie-beam and two
capitals of the
ambulatory

with the full tone and the half tone. For harmonization of its chords, it utilizes the tetrachords of Greek origin.

Traditional musical instruments include the *qassaba* and the *nay*–two varieties of short-reed wood instruments, the first having five apertures and the second seven.

Another instrument is the *rababa*–a one-string instrument with a square body and straight neck. The *rababa* was originally played by the Bedouin but has been replaced, in modern compositions, by the *kamanja* (violin).

The *oud* (lute) is a pear-shaped instrument with five double strings played with a slip of an eagle's feather.

The *qanun* is an Oriental instrument, similar to the European zither, with twenty-six strings, fitted over a flat trapezoid box and played with two metal plectra attached to the index fingers.

Of percussion instruments there are the *daff*, or *riqq*, a circular tambourine, and the *durbakkeh*, a clay vase-shaped drum with a skin drumhead.

The traditional musical ensemble is the *takht*, which has more vocal than instrumental elements. Radio Jordan's *takht* is the most prominent; it gives stage performances and participates in festivals. The armed forces and the Public Security Department have their own bands which have acquired international fame. Jordanian military bands have participated in many international contests and won first prize in an international festival in London in 1955 and at the Bari International Festival in 1961.

Attempts have been made to modernize Jordanian music. These were started by two Palestinian composers who favoured Western classical styles based on Arabic themes. In 1969 there followed four pieces for piano and in 1972, a piano sonata. Musical works composed for the orchestra included the *Jerusalem Symphony*, the *Hussein Ibn Ali Symphony* and the *Hussein Ibn Talal Symphony*.

Musical education is provided by the Music Institute, established in 1966 by the Department of Culture and Arts to foster an appreciation of music and to school amateurs in its various branches. Full-time regular students are enrolled to study

77

Western and Oriental music for a period of three years, after which they are granted the Secondary Music Certificate. Higher studies for a period of two years are offered to exceptional students, who qualify for the Diploma of the Institute.

Folk dancing and folk music often go hand in hand and in Jordan the most popular dance is the *dabkeh* in which participants line side by side and follow the movements of the leader. The *dabkeh* is usually performed to the accompaniment of the *mijwiz* (twin-piked flute) or the *nay*.

In 1966, the Department of Culture and Arts formed the Jordanian Folklore Troupe in a bid to promote interest in folk dancing. The troupe performs dances taken from villages and adapted to the stage. It has performed in many world capitals, won prizes in international folklore festivals and appeared at 'Jordanian nights' sponsored by the Ministry of Tourism and Antiquities in major cities throughout the world. It has also taken part in local festivals.

The film industry in Jordan is still very new and feeling its way. Its first production was *Struggle in Jerash*, made in 1951. The second was *Jordan, My Beloved Country*, and the third was *The Snake*. In 1977 a joint Jordanian–Turkish production, *The Eagle of the East*, made quite a stir.

Archaeological museums are administered by the Department of Antiquities. There are five such museums. The Jordan Archaeological Museum in Amman and the Jerusalem Archaeological Museum contain antiquities from different parts of the Kingdom. Museums in Petra, Madaba and Karak contain items discovered in those areas.

In 1972 the Department of Antiquities founded a Mosaic Gallery, which contains pieces from the Byzantine era which were removed from their sites in Jerash and Madaba. The department also co-operated with the University of Jordan in establishing the University Archaeological Museum and with the Jordan Folklore Society in establishing a folklore museum.

The Folklore Museum is housed by the Department of Culture and Arts. It has a collection of the traditional costumes of different parts of the country. It also exhibits items showing everyday life in the Badia (desert) and the remote villages of Jordan, as well as rugs, personal weapons, and other examples of Jordanian arts and handicrafts.

The Jordan Crafts Centre, established by a private society, displays Jordanian crafts and aims at encouraging craftsmen and helping to raise the standard of craftsmanship.

The principal crafts include weaving, done in almost every home in East Bank villages. Bedouin tribes still weave on looms using camel and goat hair, producing rugs, wall hangings, cloaks, belts, sashes and tents. Carpet weaving is practised in Madaba and Karak using dyed camel and goat hair. The decorative patterns are generally striped and the colours used are red, grey, black, white, green and blue.

On the West Bank cotton threads, dyed in Damascus, are used to produce material for national costumes.

Traditional Bedouin dress and crafts in the Folklore Museum, Amman

Pottery was revived in Palestine in 1919 with the establishment of the Jerusalem Pottery Factory. Presently the raw materials are available in the villages around Ajloun.

On the East Bank metal is worked by craftsmen who produce vases, coffee pots, pans, trays, pitchers, knives and other kitchen utensils. They are often decorated with engraved arabesque patterns. Metal jewellery such as earrings, bracelets, anklets, rings and necklaces are usually inlaid with coloured stones.

Silversmiths are centred in the major cities. The designs used are traditional, and considerably influenced by Islamic and Christian symbols.

Glass blowing has been practised for centuries in the town of Hebron. Items produced are for utilitarian as well as decorative purposes. Hebron glass chandeliers hang in the Aqsa Mosque and the Dome of the Rock and in many public buildings in Jordan. The main colours used are hazel, brown, indigo, blue and green.

The Bedouin craftsmen use goat and camel skin for the production of shoes, belts, hand-bags, chair-covers, cushions, etc. Sheepskin coats, sometimes decorated with coloured flower motifs, are worn by men in East Bank villages.

Ornamental glass and stone bead necklace of the Bedouin

The traditional art form of embroidery has been practised by local women on both East and West Banks. The original designs were geometrical, but floral designs were introduced in this century. National costumes with this colourful and rich embroidery are still worn by women in the villages of both banks.

Shell work is centred in Bethlehem and Aqaba. Small pieces of mother of pearl are combined to form religious or sacred symbols, decorative motifs applied on pastry boxes, cigarette boxes, bracelets and earrings. The shells are brought from the Red Sea or imported from abroad.

Wooden boxes, knives, daggers, olive-wood rosaries, crucifixes, figurines, vases and other decorative items are made in traditional Jordanian styles. The wood of old olive trees is used after being left to dry for two years. After carving, the wood is sandpapered and rubbed with olive oil.

The Jordan Crafts Council was established in Amman in 1973. Its aim is to promote Jordanian crafts, encourage local craftsmen, preserve local arts and crafts, and aid the continued production of items of pottery, carving, engraving, straw work, silver work, olive wood, mother of pearl, embroidery and weaving.

The public library is an old institution in the Arab–Islamic world. It developed mainly as part of the mosque and included books on religion, language, law, literature, history, the humanities and science.

Until the eighteenth century books were haphazardly preserved in libraries of old mosques and in family collections. Starting in the late nineteenth century, the cultural scene began to change and many private libraries were established and recognized by learned people. Several family libraries still exist in Jerusalem, Nablus, Hebron, Salt and Amman, while libraries belonging to churches and mosques abound.

A Libraries Division was established in 1958 and attached to the Ministry of Education. This division provides a mobile library in the District of Amman and circulating libraries in all other 15 districts. On the average, a small district has 5000 books and larger districts 40 000. The largest library of the Ministry of Education is that of the Teachers' Training Institute in Amman which has 25 000 volumes.

The first public library was established in 1957 in the city of Irbid. This was followed in 1960 by the largest public library in Jordan–the Amman Municipality Library which is also the depository library for UNESCO publications. Many of these public libraries have a children's section.

Academic libraries include the University of Jordan library, the library at Yarmouk University and libraries of the three teacher training institutes attached to the Ministry of Education.

The library of the University of Jordan has 185 000 volumes and subscribes tp 700 foreign and 300 Arabic periodicals. Its new building can accommodate 300 000 titles and has a seating capacity for 600 students. It is the depository library for United Nations documents and has microfilming equipment.

There are also specialist libraries attached to institutions and government departments. Such libraries offer services to the employees and interested researchers. Among these are the libraries at the Royal Scientific Society (20 000 volumes), the Natural Resources Authority (12 000 volumes), the Central Bank (5000 volumes), the Jordan Television Corporation, Radio Jordan, the Ministry of Culture and the Ministry of Information.

Most of the foreign cultural centres maintain their own libraries. The oldest and largest is the British Council Library in Amman established in 1950. It houses 17 000 volumes and subscribes to 120 periodicals.

The Jordan Library Association was established in 1963 and its membership in 1977 totalled 420. It has been a member of the International Federation of Libraries Association (IFLA) since 1967.

This association publishes a quarterly review *Risalat Al Maktabah (News from the Library)* and periodic bibliographies. It also offers courses to about forty trainees annually.

9 Press and Information

Mass communication media in Jordan consist of radio, television, newspapers, magazines and various periodicals. The area is organized by the government and by private enterprise: newspapers and periodicals are privately owned and published, while the government maintains the Jordan News Agency (JNA), Radio Jordan, also known as the Hashemite Broadcasting Service (HBS), and the Jordan Television Corporation (JTV).

These three departments are directly responsible to the Minister of Information.

The press, on the other hand, represents public opinion and is in private hands. All newspapers are subject to the Press and Publications Law.

When the Amirate of Transjordan was established in 1921, there were no daily newspapers of any sort in the country, and Jordanians resorted to newspapers, magazines and other periodicals published in Palestine, Syria and Egypt.

The first government publication was a weekly newspaper—*Al Shark Al Arabi*—which first appeared in 1923. It contained official announcements, legislation, local and international news and literary and political articles. By 1929, it had developed into the government's Official Gazette and contained only official announcements, regulations and legislation.

Several weekly newspapers appeared in Jordan but most of them were short-lived. Special mention must be given to *Al Urdun* which outlived all its contemporaries and is still published. It appeared initially in Haifa (Palestine) in 1909, and in June 1927 was transferred to Amman where it was published weekly until 1949 when it appeared daily. *Al Wafa* was another weekly newspaper published in Amman for almost ten years (1938–47). *Al Jazireh* appeared first in Damascus, and then moved in 1939 to Amman where it was published sometimes daily and sometimes weekly until it ceased to publish early in 1945.

Events in Palestine had their impact on Jordan. Two well-established daily newspapers, *Falastin* founded in 1911, and *Al Difa'* founded in 1933, moved from Jaffa (which fell to the Israelis in early 1948) to the Arab City of Jerusalem, and both began to appear daily. *Al Difa'* ceased to publish early in 1967 but emerged again in 1968 until it ceased to publish in 1970. *Al Jihad*, another daily, was founded in Jerusalem during 1953. These three papers, together with *Al Manar* founded in 1960, formed Jordan's press for many years.

Early 1967 witnessed a press merger: *Falastin* and *Al Manar* were combined to become *Ad Dustour*, published in Amman by the Jordan Press and Publishing Company. Concurrently *Al Jihad* became *Al Quds* in Arab Jerusalem until the city's occupation by the Israelis in June 1967.

The Jordan Earth Satellite Station provides direct telephone and cable links with Europe and the United States and receives the Middle East's only live colour television from abroad

The daily newspaper *Al Ra'i* was first published in 1971 by the Jordan Press Foundation. In 1972 it became the organ of the Arab National Union, Jordan's only political organization, and in 1974 it became a public company of which the government owned 40 per cent of the shares. By 1975 it was completely in the hands of the private sector.

While all national newspapers are essentially political in nature, they deal, nevertheless, with such subjects as the arts, sports, business, industry, social services, education and science. Circulation for the dailies range between 6000 and 60 000 copies, while the weeklies sell anywhere between 2000 and 13 000 copies each. All newspapers sell for 50 fils an issue.

In 1977, there were six daily newspapers: *Al Urdun (Jordan)*, founded in 1909, published by Dr Hanna Khalil Nasr; *Ad Dustour (The Constitution)*, established in 1967, published by the Jordan Press and Publications Company; *Al Ra'i (Opinion)*, founded in 1971, published by the Jordan Press Foundation; *Al Akhbar (News)*, founded in 1976, published by the Arab Press Company; *Ash Sha'ab (People)*, founded in 1976, published by Dar Ash Sha'ab Press, Printing and Publishing Distribution Company; and the *Jordan Times* (in English), founded in 1975, published by the Jordan Press Foundation.

The following weekly newspapers are also owned and operated by the private sector: *Akhbar Al Usbou'* since 1959; *Amman Al Masa'* since 1962; *Al Hawadeth* since 1963; *Al Sahafi* since 1964; and *Al Liwa'* since 1972. The government owns and operates one weekly newspaper, *Al Aqsa*, published by the armed forces.

All daily and weekly newspapers are published in Amman and circulate throughout Jordan. Outside the country Jordanian newspapers circulate mainly in Lebanon, Saudi Arabia and the Arabian Gulf states.

Non-Jordanian newspapers and periodicals in Arabic, English and other languages are available in Jordan. These are brought by air, mainly from Lebanon, Britain and the USA.

There are 31 official periodicals in Jordan, classified as 'general', 'specialist', 'trade' and 'professional'. These include religious publications, children's magazines, and journals specializing in finance, economics, health, politics, youth and sport, public security, culture and the arts; in addition cultural societies, trade unions, the army and various other associations, produce their own regular publications.

Most periodicals are published by government departments in Amman and circulate throughout the Kingdom. Circulation outside Jordan is on the whole restricted to two magazines, *Al Tanmiya* (specializing in economic and social development), published by the Ministry of Information, and *Afkar*, a quarterly cultural magazine published by the Department of Culture and Arts.

The Jordanian constitution grants freedom of expression to all citizens 'except in cases of emergency or martial law when a limited censorship may be imposed on newspapers, pamphlets, books, and broadcasts in matters relating to public security and national defence'.

The Jordan News Agency (JNA) was established in 1965 to publish and distribute news and features on the various activities in the country. It operates a teleprinter network, which relays news to local newspapers, government departments and Jordan's embassies abroad. The JNA has offices and correspondents in all Jordanian cities. It also maintains bureaux in Beirut and Cairo.

To widen the sphere of activities of the Jordan News Agency and to cope with modern developments in mass media techniques, it has been decided to construct new transmitters capable of world-wide coverage. Early in 1974, work began on the construction of two 10 Kilowatt HF transmitters that would cover teleprinter services to Damascus, Baghdad, Kuwait, Jeddah, Riyadh, Cairo, Khartoum, Tripoli (Libya), Tunis, Algeria, Rome, Paris, Bonn, London and New York.

The Jordan Press Association was established on 16 March 1969. This body has 150 members, including apprentice journalists; it concerns itself with professional standards and problems. The association is a member of the Jordan Professional Union, the Arab Press Association and the International Press Association. It is directed by a Press Council, and is presided over by a president who is elected every two years.

Broadcasting by radio and television in Jordan is regulated by the Ministry of Information. Two public bodies–the Jordan Television Corporation (JTV) and Radio Jordan–are the only licensed bodies to offer broadcasting services.

Both Radio Jordan and the Jordan Television Corporation are required to provide the public with information, education and entertainment. They are independent bodies in their day-to-day broadcasting, programming and administration. Each is administered by a Director General, who is responsible to the Minister of Information for the execution of the policy guidelines laid down for the broadcasting service. The government retains supervisory control and the Minister of Information is responsible to Parliament on general questions of policy. Both organs are expected to show balance and impartiality in their general presentation of programmes, particularly where matters of public policy or controversial issues are concerned; both prepare annual reports and financial statements for presentation to the Cabinet.

In 1948, with the establishment of the State of Israel, Arab employees of the Palestine Broadcasting Service (PBS), which had been founded in 1936 by the British Mandatory Government, rallied to the Jordanian military authorities in Palestine and broadcast from studios in the PBS transmission premises in Ramallah. When the West Bank united with Jordan in 1950, the radio station at Ramallah became the 'Broadcasting Service of the Hashemite Kingdom of Jordan'. At that time, thirteen hours of programmes were broadcast daily over a 20 000 watt medium-wave transmitter used previously by the PBS.

The need soon arose for a central station in Amman, the seat of government. A modern building, housing the nucleus of the present radio compound, was inaugurated on 1 March 1959.

In the past eighteen years, Radio Jordan has developed into a modern service, pioneering such fields as in-service training and the export of skilled personnel to newly established radio stations throughout the Arab world, especially in the Arab Gulf area.

At present Radio Jordan transmits about thirty-three hours daily over nine transmitters with a total power of 430 000 watts. Programmes are broadcast on FM and medium wave for listeners in Jordan and the neighbouring Arab countries, and on short wave to listeners in North America, Europe, North Africa and the Arab Gulf.

A recent survey showed that 98 per cent of Jordan's population tune in regularly to Radio Jordan's programmes, especially to news bulletins and current events programmes. To give up-to-the-minute news coverage and analysis, Radio Jordan maintains correspondents within the Kingdom and abroad.

Work has been in progress since 1972 on the construction of two medium-wave 1·2 megawatt transmitters. The project aims to expand transmission to neighbouring Arab countries. Day coverage will include Lebanon, Syria and Egypt, while night coverage will also include Iraq, Kuwait, Saudi Arabia, Libya and Tunis. This new broadcasting station went into operation at the end of 1978.

This broadcasting 'overspill' is very common in the Middle East owing to the proximity of capitals where radio stations are usually located. Thus geography and competition are important considerations, and a constant challenge to programme directors. The combined power of the two 1·2 megawatt transmitters will enable Radio Jordan's coverage to be increased in the countries of the Middle East during the day, and the wider Arab world at night.

In 1977 Radio Jordan was broadcasting 140 hours a week in Arabic to the Near East, North Africa, Europe and the Western Hemisphere. English-language programmes were broadcast for $12\frac{1}{2}$ hours daily to listeners in Jordan, Europe and North America.

The programme output is equally divided between information and education programmes and those designed for entertainment. Surveys and letters from listeners throughout the Arab world (where reception is usually good), and from foreign countries (which receive Radio Jordan's signal through a number of short-wave beams), indicate that the present policy of concentrating on news, current events and special features is very popular.

Radio Jordan presents twelve daily news bulletins in Arabic and five in English.

General view of the
control room of the
Hashemite
Broadcasting Station

Reading the news in
the Radio Jordan
studios

These bulletins, ranging in duration from five to ten minutes each, cover local, regional and international news.

The General Home Service–twenty hours daily–is broken down according to programme content, in the following manner:

Arabic service programme output in hours per week

News, current events and political commentaries	15	*per cent*
Cultural programmes and drama	10	
Special audience programmes	10	
Religious programmes	12	
Farm and development programmes	5	
Variety	20	
Music	28	

A two-year plan has been devised to boost the English-language transmission to twenty hours daily with emphasis on news and music.

Radio Jordan provides listeners with two channels, each with a distinctive character. It uses seven studios (to be increased to nine fully equipped studios by the end of 1978) and two mobile units. It has four medium-wave transmitters and four short-wave transmitters. Two FM stereo transmitters were put into service in 1974.

Commercial announcements are carried on the Arabic service only on a limited basis, to help cover costs. The content of advertisement is screened by a special panel to conform with the rigorous standards laid down by the Ministry of Information.

Radio Jordan is a member of the International Telecommunications Union (ITU). This international body promotes the development of technical media and improves telecommunication services throughout the world. Jordan adheres to ITU regulations regarding the allocation of frequencies, to eliminate interference among stations, and achieve the maximum utility of the radio spectrum.

Radio Jordan is also a member of the European Broadcasting Union (EBU), which was established to advance international broadcasting projects. It is a founding member of the Arab States Broadcasting Union (ASBU), which supervises programme exchanges among radio stations in the Arab world. ASBU also has a sixty-minute programme, produced in rotation by various radio stations in the Arab world and broadcast simultaneously by them all once every month as part of a pan-Arab policy.

The ASBU General Council agrees on a general topic for each year's programmes. Programmes for the year 1976/7 concentrated on the problems of youth in each of the participating Arab countries.

Radio Jordan exchanges programmes with a number of broadcasting organizations around the world including the BBC, the Deutsche Welle, Radio Moscow, the Japanese Broadcasting Service (NHK), the French Organization of Radio and Television (ORTF) and Radio Finland, as well as UNESCO Radio and the radio services of other specialist UN agencies.

Radio Jordan has participated in many international contests, including the annual 'Melodies of Asia' competitions in which a Jordanian folk tune won first prize in 1962.

Inside the studios of
Jordan Television
Right: The inaugura-
tion of Jordan
Television in 1968

The Television Corporation Act of 1968 authorized the Ministry of Culture and
Information to set up a special corporation to take charge of 'the establishment of
television in the Kingdom, its management, development, maintenance, and any
other works or duties pertaining to its operation'.

Although the Jordan Television Corporation (JTV) adheres to the general
policy guidelines followed by all governmental agencies, its financial and administrative independence ensures its autonomy in programming. Its stated aim is 'to
make available to the citizens of Jordan information to enable them to be fully
aware of the world they live in, by educating them, by helping them to develop
their potential for reasoning and wise judgement, by fostering their appreciation
of art, and by offering them wholesome entertainment'.

Jordan Television was inaugurated in April 1968 with a daily four-hour
transmission in black and white. Today Jordanians can watch two different all-
colour programmes; colour television transmission was introduced on the basis
of the PAL system in April 1974. The General Programme is carried on Channel
3 for six hours daily (fourteen hours on Friday), and the Foreign Programme is
carried on Channel 6 for four hours daily, including two news bulletins, one in
Hebrew and the other in English. Surveys show that Jordan TV is considered
one of the most effective in the Middle East.

The ownership of a television receiving set is subject to an annual licence fee
of JD 6 (US $20, £15). At the end of 1976, it was estimated that there were
120 000 television and 521 000 radio sets in the country.

When Jordan Television began operation, advisers from the USA, Great
Britain, Germany and Japan were assigned to help train members of the staff in
various technical areas. Twenty-five Jordanians were sent on scholarships in the
early days of Jordan Television to the USA, Great Britain, Germany, France and

Lebanon for training. As a result, Jordan Television has become the main supplier of skilled manpower for television stations in a number of Arab countries.

The role of television in Jordan is shaped by a philosophy of public service rather than pure entertainment. Television is regarded as the medium with the greatest potential for the promotion of education in the country, and this attitude is reflected in the programming.

Locally produced programmes and news take 37 per cent of transmission time, imported Arabic programmes, 14 per cent, and foreign imported programmes, 49 per cent.

The News Department broadcasts five bulletins daily (two in Arabic, one in English, one in French, and one in Hebrew). The bulletins are totally non-commercial and bring to viewers the fullest coverage of international and local news. International news films are received from international television news agencies, as well as the Jordan Satellite Earth Station at Baqa'a, outside Amman.

In the first year of Jordan Television's operation it was agreed with the Ministry of Education to produce instructional programmes, mainly for the second and third years of the secondary level, in Arabic, English, geography, physics and mathematics. In this endeavour Jordan Television puts at the disposal of the Ministry of Education its technical expertise and studio facilities, while the ministry provides trained teachers with professional knowledge in educational television, to plan, prepare and develop programmes.

Commercial advertising is viewed as an additional source of income for the corporation. At present, advertising is limited to ten or fifteen minutes of each day's broadcasting. There are plans, however, to double the present advertising time. Arrangements are being made to encourage international firms to advertise on Jordan Television to reach the increasing number of viewers in Jordan and the neighbouring countries.

JTV is an active member of the European Broadcasting Union (EBU) with all the rights, duties and responsibilities that this entails, particularly in the activities of Eurovision. The EBU is responsible for technical and administrative arrangements in co-ordinating the exchange of programmes over that network and for intercontinental satellite links. Jordan is a pioneer in the Arab world in making full use of the satellite–and in helping neighbouring countries make use of it through its position as a centre of international news relays via satellite in the Middle East. Jordan Television is also a member of the Asian Broadcasting Union (ABU).

Phosphates crushing and screening plant. Jordan's dramatic industrial expansion is

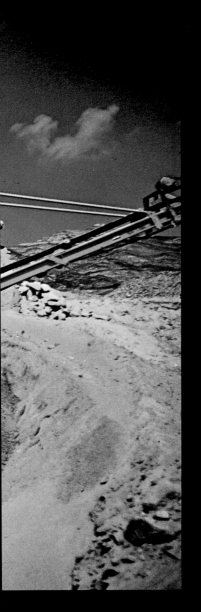

PART THREE
Looking to the Future

10 Education

While Jordan has a population of less than three million, it makes up in quality what it lacks in quantity. Its citizens are among the best educated and most talented people in the Middle East. Education is a priority on which the Jordanian government spends 8 per cent of its annual budget. Skills are among the country's chief exports. Half the population is under fifteen and every third person is a student. King Hussein has often referred to his subjects, and particularly to the youth, as 'Jordan's richest resource'.

The present educational system was founded after the Hashemite Kingdom was established in 1946 on a basis inherited from earlier years.

Before 1921 Transjordan had a traditional system of education. A legacy of the Ottoman regime, it was restricted to a few Muslim religious schools known as *kuttabs* and a handful of elementary schools. Immediately after the founding of the Amirate a comprehensive education programme was launched, and in 1922 the number of schools had risen to 44, with 71 teachers.

In May 1923 the foundation stone of the Sultanic (secondary) school was laid in Salt, and the first conference of teachers in Transjordan was held there in the summer of that year. Curricula in all government schools were unified in August 1923, following the establishment of the country's first Education Council.

Intermediate secondary schools were established in the towns of Salt, Irbid, Amman, and Karak. Later the schools in Salt and Irbid were upgraded to full secondary schools. By 1930/1 there were 5239 pupils in 54 government schools with 122 teachers, and the budget had risen to around 23 500 Palestinian Pounds—6·3 per cent of the total government budget. The present Industrial Secondary School at Amman was established in 1930 as a trade school, accepting students who had completed their elementary studies but were unable to join the available secondary schools.

The first Ministry of Education, established on 24 September 1940, laid down the education structure of the Amirate. This consisted of a seven-year elementary cycle and a four-year secondary cycle, as well as a technical cycle (trades and agriculture) comprising a two-year course. There were two government-sponsored general examinations: the first at the end of the elementary cycle and the second at the end of the secondary cycle.

The story of education in Palestine between 1919 and 1950 was different. In 1914, there was only one school (in Jerusalem) offering complete secondary education. Two schools, one in Acre and the other in Nablus, offered intermediate secondary education. There were, however, about 500 primary schools run by private national societies as well as by foreign missionary and other organizations:

Campus life,
University of Jordan

95

American, German, British, French, Italian and Russian. There were also teacher training colleges run by the Russians and Germans.

During the British Mandate, established in 1920 a number of elementary and secondary schools were built. By the time the Mandate ended in 1948, there were 250 elementary schools, 20 intermediate schools and 4 full secondary schools, each offering studies in one of the following specialisations: commerce, industrial trades, agriculture and an academic subject.

With the unification of the East and West Banks of the Kingdom in 1950, all schools were placed under the direct supervision and control of the Ministry of Education in Amman. The ministry's first major step was to divide the country into six educational districts: Nablus, Jerusalem, Hebron, Ajloun, Balq'a and Karak – the first three in the West Bank, the second three in the East Bank. In 1950, the total number of schools was 691, with 123,319 pupils and 3,022 teachers. In the school year 1979-80 the number of schools in the East Bank offering general education was 2,617, with 403 second-shift schools, and there were 704,334 pupils in those schools, and 25,802 teachers. The first 'Schools Ordinance', regulating the organisation of schools and the examination system, was published in 1952.

Education in Jordan is provided by both the public and the private sector. Schools at the elementary, preparatory and secondary levels, as well as institutes of higher education, are mostly run by the Ministry of Education, with most kindergartens run by the private sector. The Ministry of Defence, the Ministry of Public Health, the Ministry of Social Development, UNRWA, the Ministry of Waqf, the Ministry of Industry and Commerce and the Royal Scientific Society also run schools and training programmes. UNRWA (the United Nations Relief and Works Agency) provides education for about 131,000 pupils. Private schools cater for about 68,000 pupils. There are also two universities, the University of Jordan and Yarmouk University, with a third one in the planning stage.

Education in Jordan is free and compulsory in the first nine grades; and it is free in both types of secondary education, general and vocational, and in teacher training institutes and the Higher Institute of Agriculture. Boarders in vocational schools and higher educational institutes board free of charge. Textbooks are free to pupils in elementary and preparatory schools, and are available at cost price in secondary schools.

The Ministry of Education receives financial support from both the central and local government. Education receives 7.49 per cent of the national budget at present, and the Ministry's expenditure in 1979 was nearly JD 36 million.

Pre-school education commences at the age of three. In 1979-80 there were 189 kindergartens in the East Bank, with 17,160 pupils and 639 teachers.

Children are admitted to the first grade of elementary school at the age of six, and the elementary cycle lasts for six years. Here the child learns Arabic, religion, arithmetic, civics, geography, science (starting in the fifth grade), drawing (for boys), embroidery (for girls), music and physical education. From the fifth grade on, all children take English as their second language for five periods a week. About a third of the elementary schools are co-educational, and boys and girls are approximately equal in numbers in elementary school enrolment.

One characteristic of elementary education in Jordan is the system of modified automatic promotion. A child is permitted to repeat a grade once in the entire six

Refugee children flock to school. Schools administered by UNRWA follow the Ministry of Education curriculum. Today Jordan's literacy rate is one of the highest in the area

years of study, after which promotion to a higher grade is automatic.

In 1979-80 there were 448,411 pupils and 13,898 teachers at 1,095 elementary schools in the East Bank.

Most pupils are promoted from the sixth to the seventh grade and start the three-year preparatory cycle at the age of twelve.

In the school year 1979-80 there were 158,590 pupils and 7,619 teachers at 992 preparatory schools in the East Bank. In 1976 the Ministry of Education decided to abolish the general preparatory examination at the end of the preparatory cycle, and to give the responsibility for evaluating the pupils to the schools.

At the end of these nine years of compulsory education, pupils can go on to their secondary education at vocational (industrial, agricultural or commercial) or academic schools, depending on the pupil's preference, the evaluation of the pupil's ability, and the number of places available in the various types of secondary schools.

The secondary education cycle in Jordan consists of the tenth, eleventh and twelfth grades. Secondary schools are of three types: the general, the vocational and the comprehensive. In the first year of the three-year cycle, all pupils follow the same curriculum. In the second year, pupils in general schools and classes separate into arts and sciences streams. An average of 34 in every 100 pupils entering secondary schools reach the third year of the cycle. At the end of the secondary cycle all pupils sit for the public secondary education examination, success in which qualifies them to continue their education in Jordan or abroad.

In 1979-80 there were over 90,000 pupils and 4,289 teachers in 357 secondary schools in the East Bank.

From 1977 the school year has been divided into semesters and seminar courses have been available for pupils wishing to take them.

The educational programme provided for the Palestine Arab refugees in Jordan is the responsibility of the United Nations Relief and Works Agency for Palestine Refugees (UNRWA) and the United Nations Educational, Scientific and Cultural Organization (UNESCO). UNRWA is responsible for the administration of the programme while UNESCO assumes the technical responsibility. This arrange-

Analysing a mineral sample in the laboratories of Jordan University
Left: Skilled worker operating a machine lathe. There are more than thirty vocational training centres in the country

ment dates from the start of UNRWA's activities in 1950. UNRWA schools follow the same curriculum and use the same textbooks as those of the Ministry of Education. In 1977 there were 192 UNRWA schools.

UNRWA also operates five vocational training centres. Training consists of two programmes: one at secondary level and the other at post-secondary level.

There are seven teacher training institutes on the East Bank. Four of them are run by the Ministry of Education, one by UNRWA, and two by the private sector. They supply teachers for elementary and preparatory schools. Attached to each is a research college to carry out experiments in new fields of education, especially methodology, and to enable students to practise teaching. Holders of the secondary education certificate are eligible for admission.

A determined campaign is currently in progress to overcome illiteracy. In 1961, according to the census of that year, the rate of illiteracy was 67·5 per cent. A pilot project lasting nine months was launched in November 1965 with highly encouraging results. Since 1966 the literacy campaign has been a permanent feature. The course it offers covers two years, based on an eight-month academic year. A recent survey on the population provides further information on the educational standards of married persons of fifteen years of age and above. It shows that the rate of illiteracy in Jordan was 38 per cent in 1974. Today Jordan's literacy rate is one of the highest in the area–65 per cent and rising.

The possibilities of television as an educational aid have long been recognized. Introduced by the Ministry of Education in 1968 for instruction in secondary schools in English, science, mathematics and physics to the eleventh grade, educational programmes are televised three times a week. Television sets have been installed in more than forty secondary schools throughout the six educational districts of the Kingdom.

In 1969 the Board of Education was established to ensure stability and continuity of educational policy and the smooth running of the system. The board makes recommendations on the implementation of general educational policy, studies the annual budget of the Ministry of Education and presents its recommendations, and offers the ministry expert advice on the establishment of new educational

University students
use electronic
microscopes to examine
slide-specimens
Right : Every year King
Hussein personally
bestows degrees on
University of Jordan
graduates

institutions. However, its most important function is in laying down the basic guidelines to be followed in the construction and design of curricula and textbooks.

In the sphere of higher education, many students, both at home and abroad, have Jordanian government scholarships. There are 1268 students studying at the ministry's expense, of whom 990 are either at the University of Jordan or Yarmouk University and 278 are studying abroad.

The two universities crown the country's education system. The University of Jordan is an autonomous body, governed by a Board of Trustees consisting of ten members of high calibre and status who represent various sections of Jordanian society. The university has a council composed of its president, deans of its faculties, and an elected professor who serves for a term of one year. Each faculty has a governing council composed of the dean and its professors. Students are admitted if they hold the public secondary education certificate or its equivalent. Starting with 167 boys and 18 girls and a single faculty of arts in 1962, the university today has well over 5000 students, of whom more than a third are women. About 80 per cent of the professors are Jordanian, products of earlier stages of the country's educational work. The faculties cover the arts, science, economics and commerce, medicine, nursing, agriculture, psychology, education and engineering. The faculty of religion is served by the College of Shari'a, which grants a BA degree in the subject.

In order to provide additional accommodation for qualified students seeking higher education, a royal decree was issued on 1 June 1975 establishing Jordan's second university, the Yarmouk University, in the northern part of the country. A royal commission was appointed to act as the Board of Trustees. Instruction at Yarmouk started in the academic year of 1976/7. Faculties and departments comprise science and the arts, engineering, medicine, agriculture and veterinary medicine, a unit for research and graduate studies, and a new law college.

11 Planning for Progress

Jordan's East Bank population is, according to the 1979 census, 2.2 million and is increasing at an annual rate of 3.8%. The west Bank of Jordan has remained under Israeli occupation since 1967. Besides, about a quarter of a million Jordanians are working abroad.

Growth in population, more paved streets and busier traffic are, however, only a surface measure of a nation's progress. To gauge the true quality and extent of development that has occurred in Jordan, one must look to all sections of its life, to the combined achievements of its government and its people. The evidence is all about, in the new schools and hospitals, in the rapidly expanding economy, in business, industry and agriculture, in the modern transportation and communication networks that web the country, and in the enriched cultural life of its society.

Jordan is not an oil producing country. It has also to import most of its basic requirements. All Jordan's development plans have consequently aimed at reducing the trade deficit and increasing economic self-sufficiency.

The country's monetary unit is the Jordan dinar, equivalent to about US$ 3.00. The dinar is divided into 1000 fils or, more popularly, 100 piastres.

Recent studies of the economy point to two main areas of productive potential. One is the full utilization of the Jordan Valley water resources for irrigation. The other is the exploitation of mineral deposits, particularly of phosphates, potash, copper and limestone. With recent projects to utilize these mineral reserves Jordan will soon be in a position to operate sizable and sophisticated fertilizer and chemical industries.

Computer in the laboratories of the Royal Scientific Society. This is Jordan's 'think tank', established in 1970 to conduct research into the problems arising from the country's rapid transition to the technological age

The greater utilization of Jordan's natural and human resources, however, would not only accelerate the development of the other sectors of the economy and improve the well-being of its citizens; it would finally bring the country fiscal self-reliance, and contribute to the prosperity and progress of the Arab world as a whole.

In the last 3 decades Jordan has made remarkably rapid economic and social progress. This was achieved in spite of enormous population pressures and capital scarcities particularly as a result of events in Palestine.

The Gross National Product (GNP) at current market prices stood at JD 1011 million in 1980 and average per capita income at JD 453. During the period of the Five Year Plan 1976-80, GNP increased in current prices at an annual rate of 24.2%, agriculture at 18.1%, industry at 27% (industrial production index at 18.3) and the services sector at 19.4%, exports at 26.8% and imports at 25.2%. The ratio of investments in relation to GNP at factor cost also rose from 25 percent in 1975 to 33 percent during the Plan period.

These figures indicate a considerable rise in the standard of living as well as rapid expansion in the capacity of the economy to produce goods and services both for domestic use and export. Saving and investment showed a significant increase, while at the same time the economy made strides towards self-sufficiency.

Agriculture is still an important feature of the economy. It engages about one-fifth of the working population and contributes about one-tenth of the Gross Domestic Product (GDP). The value of agricultural production increased from JD 26 million in 1975 to JD 60 million in 1980.

Due to increased plantation of olives, grapes and citrus, vegetable production has greatly increased so that Jordan is now not only self-sufficient in these crops but exports sizable amounts to neighbouring and distant markets. In recent years, the exports of fruits and nuts and vegetables has exceeded 25% of the value of total exports.

To reduce agriculture's dependence upon rainfall, which in the past has been erratic, resulting in severe fluctuations in output and income, emphasis was given to irrigation schemes and soil and water conservation. To this end, the East Ghor Canal was constructed, diverting the waters of the Yarmouk River to irrigate lands in the Jordan Valley by gravity flow. This was the first stage in a major scheme aimed at harnessing the waters of the Yarmouk River through construction of the Maqarin dam.

Meanwhile, special attention was given to the social aspects of agricultural development through the establishment and strengthening of the important co-operative movement. There are now 141 agricultural and 173 non-agricultural co-operatives with a membership of 12,000 and 17,000 respectively. The Jordan Co-operative Organization provides loans, supervision, advice and auditing services to local co-operatives.

In 1960 the Agricultural Credit Corporation was created to give loans to farmers and to finance agricultural investments, particularly those aimed at improving efficiency and expanding production. The outstanding loans of JCO to co-operatives in 1980 was JD 8 million, and that of ACC JD 13 million.

In the industrial sector the rate of development has been no less impressive. The share of mining and manufacturing in GDP in current prices increased from JD 47 million in 1975 to JD 154 million in 1980.

Two large cement factories, a petroleum refinery, a number of foundries, a tannery, several marble factories and phosphate-mining plants are already in operation. The large industrial projects now under implementation include a JD 160 million potash scheme at the Dead Sea, a JD 120 million fertilizer plant, a JD 140 million investment for 3 cement plants, a JD 60 million expansion of the petroleum refinery and a JD 60 million expansion of phosphate mining, excluding the considerable investment foreseen for the development of the Shidiya deposits. Other industrial activities include milling, oil pressing, textiles, bottling, brewing, tobacco products, footwear, metal products, furniture, detergents, food products, batteries, glass, printing and publishing.

According to the Industrial Survey of 1979 there were 2,644 manufacturing establishments employing 29,123 persons. The value of their production was JD 249.7 million, and the average productivity was JD 8,575 per worker.

In July 1965, the Industrial Development Bank was established. It has an authorized capital of JD 6 million, of which JD 1 million has been subscribed by the government and JD 3 million by the private sector. The bank aims to hasten indu-

Oil refinery near Zarqa

Right: Confectionary factory at Khirbat Abu Nasr
Far right: Modern ceramics and china plant

strial development by offering medium and long-term loans, and providing technical assistance and advice.

Extensive geological surveys led to the discovery of large deposits of phosphates which had been exploited for over three decades.

Several surveys have proved the existence of minerals such as iron, lead sulphide, tin, granite, pyrite, molybdenum, decorative marble rocks and gypsum. Detailed studies on their characteristics are now under way. Besides, studies have been made on oil exploration including seismic, gravity and magnetic surveys as an integrated programme for development of energy sinne Jordan wholly depends on imported crude oil. They have proven the existence of large quantities of oil shale and further studies are being made to evaluete their economic exploitation.

Electricity power generation has increased from 374 gigawatt hours in 1975 to 1068 gigawatt hours in 1980. The percentaoe of population supplied with electricity through electric networks rose from 39% in 1975 to 65% in 1980. Per capita consumption of electricity rose from 209 KWH in 1975 to 478 KWH in 1980.

The tourist industry saw phenomenal expansion during recent years. The annual number of tourists visiting Jordan has exceeded the one million mark. The 1967 war and the consequent loss of Jerusalem end other cities of the West Bank severely depressed the industry, but the government did not lose heart. The expansion of tourism was given high priority in Jordan's development plans. The number of modern hotels was increased and roads connecting the various religious and archaeological sites were constructed to make them more accessible to visitors.

Great progress has been made in education, public health and social services. In the scholastic year of 1979/80 there were 607,000 students in the compulsory cycles (primary and preparatory) as against 398,000 in 1975/76. 97% of the age group 6-11 years are now enrolled in schools. The number of private and government hospitals and clinics increased appreciably during the same period, and the standard of medical services improved consistently. The infant mortality rate of 23 per thousand is one of the lowest among Arab countries. The average life expectancy has now increased to 58 years in comperison with 46 in 1961.

Trade and commerce, transport, and communications were given special attention. A modern and efficient system of roads and communications was constructed. The port of Aqaba, Jordan's only access to the Red Sea, was developed, and work is under way to expand its facilities to accommodate the anticipated increase in exports, especially of phosphates and potash.

Faced with a host of political, economic and military challenges, the government of Jordan managed, despite its limited financial resources, to meet its increasing responsibilities and to allocate a significant proportion of its total expenditure to development purposes. It also gave serious attention to strengthening the governmental systems so that it might play an effective role in the country's economic and social development.

The total government revenues rose from JD 213 million in 1975 to JD 500 million in 1980 of which domestic revenues constituted JD 83 million and 224 million respectively. Total government expenditures rose from JD 205 million in 1975 to JD 518 million in 1980. The ratio of current and capital expenditures of the government to GNP has averaged 33% and 20% during the last five years and the ratio of domestic revenues to current expenditures has risen from 66% in 1975 to 69% in 1980.

Traffic at Amman
International Airport, a
busy aviation centre.
A new $90 million
airport is under
construction at Giza,
south of Amman
Right : Rail
construction in the
desert. A road and
railway network spans
the country, replacing
the 'caravan' routes of
old

Jordan has long recognized the importance of long-range planning for the effective use of its resources. The aim of its Seven-Year Plan (1964-70) was to steer the country as rapidly as possible towards economic independence and sustained growth. It gave high priority to agriculture, mining, tourism and manufacturing, and called for the implementation of development projects of all kinds.

The main goals of the Seven-Year Plan, in order of importance, were as follows:

1. A major reduction in the balance of trade deficit and a major reduction in budget support;
2. An increase in per capita income, at as rapid a rate as possible, consistent with objective (1); and
3. A reduction in the level of unemployment.

The plan aimed at increasing the Gross National Product from JD 137 million in 1963 to JD 226 million in 1970, that is by about 65 percent. The second objective was to reduce the trade deficit from JD 41 million in 1963 to JD 24 million in 1970, that is from 30 percent to 11 percent of the Gross National Product. Employment opportunities were similarly programmed to increase at an annual rate exceeding 5 percent.

Jordan's steady rate of progress becomes all the more admirable in view of the disastrous consequences of the 1967 war on the nation's economy. In one sudden blow, the entire West Bank was seized, placing one-third of Jordan's population under Israeli occupation. Agricultural revenue was reduced by half, and with the loss of Jerusalem and other Holy Land sites, Jordan's principal industry, tourism, collapsed. There was also the tragic burden of 250,000 new refugees to cope with.

105

With characteristic vigour and resilience, the nation began to restore its battered economy. The interrupted Seven-Year Hlan was replaced in 1972 with a new Three-Year Plan (1973-5), which redefined development objectives and determined new strategies and policies to meet the changed situation. This plan was comprehensive in scope, flexible in nature, and constituted a guideline for Jordan's subsequent development. It was also a purely Jordanian effort and accomplishment. Participation in its preparation was widespread, involving virtually all sections of Jordanian society.

As a first step the achievements of the past were assessed and the current situation analysed. In the light of these findings, and of the country's overall economic and social objectives, the following conclusions were reached which formed the basis of the long-term strategy: the citizen was the nation's most valuable resource and asset; there should be a more democratic participation in the decision-making process and in planning and development; there would have to be closer co-operation and co-ordination between the private and public sectors; the productive sectors of the economy needed to be expanded and diversified, and foreign trade rationalized; government machinery was in need of re-structuring to make it more planning-conscious and development-orientated; and foreign capital investment in local development would have to be encouraged.

Within this framework the objectives of the Three-Year Development Plan were defined and the requisite policies determined.

The primary objective of the Plan was to reactivate the national economy and resume the development momentum which had been interrupted by the event of June 1967. The specific targets were as follows:

1. Creation of 70,000 new job opportunities.
2. Achieving an 8 per cent annual growth rate of Gross Domestic Product, and an 8.2 per cent growth rate of Gross National Product.
3. Developing economic and social activity throughout the Kingdom, with greater participation of all private and public organizations and citizens, and with heavy reliance on regional development.
4. Increasing the reliance of the general budget on domestic revenue to 53 per cent, and also accelerating the rate of increase of domestic revenues of local authorities (municipalities).
5. Strengthening the balance of payments and restraining the deficit in the trade balance. Although this deficit would increase in absolute terms its proportion to Gross National Product would be expected to decrease from 30 per cent in 1971 to 24 per cent in 1975.

The Plan recognized that the achievement of these goals required policies and measures that would create a suitable institutional framework, would modernize and improve the performance of government machinery, and would encourage private investment and manpower development. It gave priority to the development of the service and social sectors of the economy, in view of their direct contributions to employment, output and foreign exchange. To that end it called for the following actions:

1. Channelling an increasing proportion of national resources towards investment,

so that investment, as a percentage of Gross National Product, would increase from 15 per cent in 1971 to 20 per cent per annum during the period of the Three-Year Plan.

2. Investment during the Plan period of JD 179 million: JD 114 million in the economic sectors, and JD 65 million in the social sectors.
3. Public investment of JD 100 million, and private sector investment of JD 79 million.
4. Extending and deepening citizen participation by promoting private savings and investments in the productive sectors; encouraging participation in financing public projects by the purchase of treasury bills and development bonds; creating opportunities for voluntary and collective participation in public projects.
5. Developing contacts with friendly countries and international and regional agencies to procure increased technical and economic assistance.
6. Creating favourable conditions for domestic and foreign private investment by giving greater incentives to entrepreneurs and by establishing institutions to mobilize local savings.
7. Improving the efficiency of government by the introduction of modern administrative techniques and the upgrading of personnel.
8. Developing master plans in key sectors to integrate development and the phasing of activities.

In 1973 important organizational and legislative measures were put into action to implement the Plan. These included a new law to enable the Ministry of Agriculture and other agencies to introduce new agricultural methods; establishment of the Jordan Valley Commission to integrate the social and economic development of the fertile Jordan Valley area; establishment of the Industrial Development Corporation to speed up industrialization and strengthen joint ventures between the private and public sectors; a free zone at Aqaba port to be utilized among other things, to attract investment in industrial processing plants; establishment of the Housing Bank, to extend credit facilities for the construction of housing units, particularly in areas outside the overpopulated cities, and for housing co-operatives; and the conclusion of several trade agreements to improve trade relations with other countries.

The Central Bank of Jordan issued directives to commercial banks and other credit institutions to give higher priority to productive sectors such as agriculture, electricity, supply, mining, manufacturing, and the construction industry in general and tourist facilities in particular. Many corporations were established in the mining and manufacturing industries, their capital being raised from both domestic and foreign sources.

In 1973 the index of industrial production of the principal industries increased by 13.8 per cent. The combined mining and manufacturing industries' production surpassed expectations by about 15 per cent over 1972. In 1974, however, the value of industrial production increased by some 50 per cent over its 1973 level. The main reason for this great surge was the increase in the production and export prices of phosphate rock. The exports of phosphate rock constituted more than 40 per cent of total mining and manufacturing output.

Agricultural production was adversely affected by the frost and drought conditions of 1973 and 1975 and income in this sector declined by about 30 per cent of the 1972 level. In 1974 agricultural production was the highest in the 1950-74 period, estimated at more than double the 1973 level in terms of contribution to Gross Domestic Product. Wheat production declined dramatically from 211,000 tons in 1972 to about 50,000 tons in 1973, and increased to about 213,000 tons in 1974. This resulted in substantial shortages in wheat and flour during 1974, which were made up through imports.

Construction continued to expand in 1973 and 1974. The newly licensed construction areas in the three largest cities of Amman, Zarqa and Irbid recorded a rate of increase of over 50 per cent compared with 1972.

Tourist activity improved and the number of tourists in 1973 increased by about 4 per cent, from 282,600 in 1972 to 294,300 in 1973. The number of Jordanians working abroad and visiting the country also increased and contributed substantially to foreign exchange. Total income from tourism was estimated at about JD 11 million compared to JD 8.3 million for 1972.

Structural fiscal developments in 1973-75 led to substantial increases in public revenue both in absolute terms and relative to GDP. Total revenues of the central government rose from JD 93.6 million in 1972 to JD 206.7 million in 1975, or at an average rate of 30 per cent per annum.

By the end of 1975, therefore, the economy had been revitalized and the major goals of the Three-Year Plan achieved. The country was pulling itself up into prosperity.

As a result of the structural changes and the momentum achieved in the Three-Year Plan, a Five-Year Development Plan (1976-80) was initiated to carry the development drive forward. The objectives of the Five-Year Plan were as follows:

1. To realize a 12 per cent annual growth rate in Gross Domestic Product. The Plan aims to increase the GDP at 1975 prices by 75 per cent during the Plan period, from JD 290 million in 1975 to JD 508 million in 1980. This growth will be achieved by concentrating on commodity-producing sectors so as to effect a basic change in the structure of the national economy, raising the share of the commodity-production sectors in GDP from 35 percent in 1975 to 44 percent in 1980. This target is to be achieved in agriculture, manufacturing, mining, electricity and water supply, conservation and services.
2. To distribute development gains among the population in the various regions of the Kingdom, but particularly in rural areas.
3. To augment the reliance of the government budget on domestic revenues, whereby domestic revenues will grow by 115 percent during the Plan period, from JD 80 million in 1975 to JD 172 million in 1980, or at annual rates averaging 16.5 percent.
4. To reduce the trade deficit in ratio to GNP at market prices from 41.6 percent in 1975 to 20.7 percent in 1980. This reduction represents the first reversal in the trend of this economic indicator.

The attainment of these targets was based on three main assumptions: that the private sector would continue to respond to development plans by mobilizing its savings and channelling them towards investment; that the central government and municipalities would continue to direct increasing proportions of their financial resources towards investment in social overhead capital; and that Arab and other friendly countries and international agencies would respond favourably to Jordan's will and determination to accelerate its economic and social development through continuation of budget support and economic and technical assistance, and provision of concessionary loans to finance development projects.

Fixed investments during the Plan period were estimated at JD 765 million, to be divided equally between the public and private sectors.

The actual economic performance was characterized by realization of growth rates approximately close to those anticipated in the Plan. The investments amounted to JD 1222 million at current prices or equivalent to JD 844 million at 1975 prices in comparison with JD 765 million estimated in the Plan. The expenditure of the private sector exceeded the Plan estimate and accounted for 59% of total investments, and the public sector for 41%. The actual expenditure in transport, electricity and housing sectors was far above the Plan allocations. The stage of development currently attained in the several major areas of national activity has already been indicated in the earlier paragraphs of this Section. Jordan has reached full employment, – the unemployment rate is less than 2%. In fact labour shortage has arisen in some unskilled and semi-skilled categories which are now made up by foreign workers.

In order to consolidate the gains so far made and to give a further fillip to the economy to grow in the desired direction, the Five Year Plan for 1980-85 has been drafted. It will have an outlay of JD 2,800 million in current prices. The basic goals are:

1. Realizing a 10.4% annual growth rate in GDP. This means increasing the GDP at factor cost from JD 705 million in 1980 to JD 1,156 million in 1985 at 1980 prices. Annual per capita income is expected to increase at 5.3%.
2. Changing the structure of the economy in favour of commodity-producing sectors. This will be done by raising their relative share in GDP from 38.8% in 1980 to 44.8% in 1985. The annual increase in commodity sectors will be 13.5% with the services sector growing at 8.2% annually.
3. Increasing the domestic revenues of the General Budget. The ratio of domestic revenues to recurrent expenditures will increase from 70% in 1980 to 100.4% in 1985, and that of domestic revenues to GNP from 22.2% in 1980 to 35.4% in 1985.
4. Reducing the trade deficit. Imports of goods and services will increase at 11.9% yearly, and exports at 19.8% aided by expansion and diversification of domestic exports, increase in tourism and in remittances of Jordanians working abroad.
5. Providing basic needs and narrowing regional disparities through provision of industrial infrastructure and public services.
6. Developing the labour force through qualitative and quantitative improvements, increasing social security and women's participation.
7. Participating in the Arab development decade. Joint ventures will be established and unified plans promoted for development of manpower and science and technology.

Among the major policy measures are the following:

1. Increase current domestic revenues of the government by 20% annually and

restrict the annual growth in current government expenditure to 12.5% during the years 1981-1983 and to 10% during 1984 and 1985.

2. Increase the proportion of capital expenditure to total government expenditures from 37% in 1980 to an annual average of 45% during 1981-1985.

3. Increase municipal revenues by 25% annually and restrict the rate of increase in current expenditures of municipalities to 12.5% during 1981-1983 and to 10% during 1984 and 1985. Priority in municipal investments will be given to public utilities projects which generate adequate returns to augment municipal revenues.

4. Continue to secure a level of financial assistance for the general budget of at least JD 244 million.

5. Secure foreign soft loans of not less than JD 880 million during the Plan period part of which will be for financing joint projects with the private sector.

6. Eliminate gradually the subsidy from the general budget to prices of fuel and basic food commodities which amounted to JD 46 million in 1980.

Agriculture

Jordan is basically an agricultural country. Around 40 per cent of its total labour force is engaged in farming, forestry and livestock, 5 per cent of that work force being women. They contribute 18-25 per cent of the Gross Domestic Product annually. Agricultural exports represent 50 per cent of the value of the annual total. However, this sector is still unable to satisfy the country's needs for various food and agricultural products. Imports in 1975 amounted to JD 8.6 million, while exports did not exceed JD 8.4 million, a deficit in the trade balance of agricultural commodities of around JD 0.2 million.

Among the important factors affecting agriculture are climate, the nature of the terrain, the availability of water, and the level of agricultural technology.

Jordan has a dry Mediterranean climate, the temperatures rarely falling to more than a few degrees below freezing point in winter and seldom exceeding 33°C in summer.

Estimates of the possible cultivable area for Jordan were put at around 8 712 000 dunums* in 1975. However, only 32·3 per cent was actually cultivated; 9·5 per cent was fallow, and approximately 58·2 per cent was cultivable but not in use. The total number of holdings is around 50 790. About a third are less than one dunum, and another third range from 10 to 50 dunums.

The predominant form of land tenure in Jordan is that of the owner-farmer. The Agricultural Census of 1975 showed that 65 per cent of the agricultural area was operated by owners and 20 per cent by both owners and tenants, but less than 12 per cent by tenants only. Most tenancies are based on share-cropping.

Water is scarce in Jordan, and this sets a limit to the additional areas that can be cultivated and to the animal population that can be supported.

About 78 per cent of the country's total area receives an average annual rainfall of less than 200 mm, and only 1·3 per cent receives more than 600 mm. Precipitation is highly seasonal all over Jordan, being virtually confined to the winter months,

*10 dunums are equal to 1 hectare or 2½ acres.

110

The $35 million King Talal Dam will irrigate thousands of acres of prime land in the Jordan Valley and provide Amman with a reservoir

Crop-spraying with pesticides. Modern farming methods are increasingly being used

and extremely variable in amount. About 80 per cent is lost through evaporation and the remainder is lost below surface and as surface run-off. Approximately half of the area drains westwards into the Dead Sea.

The development of the water sources of the Jordan Valley was initiated in 1958, and by the end of 1973 the achievement was impressive. The following projects had been implemented: partial diversion of the waters of the Yarmouk River to the East Ghor Canal to irrigate 11 000 dunums; raising the sides of the East Ghor Canal to increase its capacity to 20 cubic metres per second; extension of the existing East Ghor Canal by 18 kilometres to irrigate an additional area of about 13 000 dunums; construction of the Wadi Ziqlab, Shueib and Kafrein dams with storage capacities of 4·3, 2·3 and 4·3 million cubic metres respectively; the preparation and partial construction of the Khalid Dam (the 1967 war brought this project to a standstill); construction of the King Talal Dam on the Zarqa River for the conservation of about 50 million cubic metres of water; the introduction of the sprinkler system of irrigation in the Zarqa triangle to irrigate about 12 000 dunums.

Suitable dam sites for the storage of surface water are relatively scarce in most areas of the Kingdom, and it is evident that the exploitation of groundwater resources is a necessity for further agricultural development. The most important groundwater sources on the East Bank are in the Jordan Valley, the North-Eastern Plateau (the Azraq, Wadi Duleil and Amman-Zarqa fields), and the South-Eastern Plateau (the Hasa, Shobak, Jafr, Wadi Arja and Rumm-Qa' Disi fields). Pilot developments of irrigated agriculture from ground resources have been initiated in several areas in East Jordan.

Although fertilizers are not used on a wide scale, owing to insufficient knowledge of their use and to their high prices, interest in their use is growing. Imports of fertilizers totalled 11 000 tons in 1975. Insecticides, herbicides and other chemicals are still used in relatively small quantities, totalling 650 tons in 1975.

The use of machines and equipment in agriculture is spreading quickly in dry-land farming. The number of tractors, fewer than 1000 in 1950, rose to 7500 in 1975. The use of other modern agricultural equipment is also expanding and replacing traditional methods. This seems to apply particularly in the case of disc ploughs, disc drillers and harvesters.

There are two main sources of agricultural credit – non-institutional and institutional. Non-institutional sources are mainly commission agents, landlords, village grocers and agricultural suppliers. This credit is mostly short term and the interest rates are high. The institutional agricultural credit system includes the two semi-autonomous agencies: the Agricultural Credit Corporation (ACC) and the Jordan Co-operative Organization (JCO). Commercial banks offer similar facilities.

The ACC was established in 1959 to be the official lending institution for agricultural purposes with an authorized capital of JD 7 million. It has sixteen branches which give long-term loans for a period not exceeding twenty years, medium-term loans for up to ten years and seasonal loans for up to one year. These are used for irrigation projects and accessories, reclamation of cultivated land through terracing and fruit tree planting, buying agricultural machinery and construction of poultry farms, farm houses, stores and stables and agricultural facilities such as olive presses. For security the ACC accepts immovable property, cash deposits, stocks and shares and bank guarantees.

There are 286 agricultural co-operative societies in Jordan whose membership amounts to 15 610 with a total capital of JD 537 000. Each is a member of the Jordan Co-operative Organization, in which the government has shares. Co-operative societies undertake only short-term financing to assist a farmer until his crop is harvested. The societies obtain funds partly from their own capital and reserves and partly from the JCO, which in turn receives global financing from the Agricultural Credit Corporation. Total outstanding loans at the end of 1973 amounted to JD 1 843 190. Lending by commercial banks totalled JD 1 811 921 in 1973, which is about 10 per cent of the amount required to meet the annual cost of agricultural production.

The rural sector in Jordan represents, to a large extent, a market economy and not a subsistence economy. Agricultural marketing officially began in 1962 when a Bureau of Agricultural Marketing was established in association with the Ministry of National Economy. Later, in 1972, the Department of Marketing was incorporated into the Directorate of Agricultural Economy in the Ministry of Agriculture. In addition to this department the Agricultural Marketing Organization is now functioning as a semi-autonomous body engaged in the search for and promotion of markets and marketing facilities, and in extending marketing services to farmers.

Agriculture is administered through a multiplicity of agencies and bodies, representing the National Planning Council (NPC), the Ministry of Agriculture, the National Resources Authority (NRA), the Agricultural Credit Corporation (ACC), the Jordan Co-operative Organization (JCO), the Agricultural Marketing Organization, the Jordan River and Tributaries Regional Corporation (JRTRC), and the Jordan Valley Commission.

Education and training in the various agricultural skills at different levels takes place inside the country as well as abroad. Part is academic and part

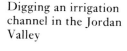

Digging an irrigation channel in the Jordan Valley

technical. While there is little formal training in agricultural skills in Jordan outside schools and institutes, the Ministry of Education has developed a system of diffusing agricultural training through the schools, and has appointed teachers with an agricultural background for this purpose. About fifty university graduates in agricultural science return to Jordan each year after being trained abroad, and recently the University of Jordan initiated a Faculty of Agriculture which awards BSc degrees in the subject.

The value of agricultural output has risen from an average of JD 20 million in the two years 1960/1 to an average of JD 37·7 million in 1972/3. The average rate of growth of agricultural output was 25·6 per cent between 1960 and 1973, while the average annual growth of Gross Domestic Product was 144·5 per cent during the same period.

The share of meat and animal products in agricultural output has risen rapidly with the rise in animal population (sheep, goats, cattle and camels). The number of slaughtered animals reached 502 308 in 1975. In the same year poultry numbered 15 560 000.

Since 1967, production has at times been hampered by the military situation in the Jordan Valley, the country's most promising agricultural area, and has also been affected by unfavourable weather conditions. The influence of these factors resulted in large variations in production from 1967 to 1976. Cereal production, wheat and barley, was 297 000 tons in 1967, 130 000 tons in 1968, 227 000 tons in 1969, 71 000 tons in 1970, 226 000 tons in 1971, 245 000 tons in 1972, 56 000 tons in 1973, 237 419 tons in 1974 and 75 705 tons in 1975. Vegetables, depending mostly on irrigation, suffered less extreme fluctuation in production, as did fruit.

Total plant production, including forest products, was 859 000 tons in 1967, 404 000 tons in 1968, 588 000 tons in 1969, 330 000 tons in 1970, 547 000 tons in 1971, 684 000 tons in 1972, 324 000 tons in 1973, 804 093 tons in 1974 and 665 369 tons in 1975.

Imports of agricultural products constitute a large part of the total imports of the country. Their average value for the period 1971–5 was JD 5·4 million (JD 8·4 million in 1975), while the average value of total domestic imports was JD 64·56 million.

The share of agricultural products in total domestic exports for the period 1967–73 averaged 50 per cent. The bulk of these exports were tomatoes, water melons, bananas and citrus fruits. Jordan's domestic exports averaged JD 5·6 million during the period 1971–5 and JD 8·6 million in 1975, while agricultural products exported averaged JD 5 million during the same period.

. Clearly Jordan is still an importer of foodstuffs and has an adverse balance of trade in agricultural produce. However development possibilities exist in all three main agricultural fields: irrigation, rainfed farming and livestock.

Irrigated farming in the lowlands of the Jordan Valley holds considerable promise. The key to this development is an increase in irrigation water, which will be made available through the new dam on the Zarqa River. To maximize economic returns from the increased irrigation water, production should be re-orientated towards citrus and other high-value fruits. Development in the rainfed areas on the other hand should aim at increasing cereal production in order to reduce imports.

Land consolidation, the storage of rainfall by soil conservation, and the application of modern cultivation methods are vital to improving cereal yields. Very little increased production can come from expanding acreage.

Jordanian agriculture is highly unstable because a large proportion of total output is derived from dryland farming in areas subject to frequent droughts. In view of the impact this has on the level of economic activity, priority has been given in the last fifteen years to irrigation schemes, soil and water conservation programmes, and the promotion of drought-resistant crops in areas where irrigation possibilities do not exist. These schemes, financed by the government, have shown steady improvement and growth.

As already pointed out, Jordan cannot satisfy its own local demand for some important agricultural products. The agricultural sector still suffers from low

The Jordan River winding along the flood plain of the Zor

Below: The Jordan Valley is the country's richest agricultural area

productivity and insufficient capital investment. In its Three-Year Plan (1973–5), the government laid great emphasis on the development of the agricultural sector through projects costing JD 27·7 million. The Plan covered irrigated farming development, dryland farming development, livestock and poultry production, forestry, soil and water development, agricultural research, and agricultural marketing measures.

Thanks to the implementation of the Three-Year Plan, agricultural income averaged approximately JD 26·4 million per annum during the period 1972–5, or 12 per cent of the Gross Domestic Product. Agricultural crops contributed 64·5 per cent of agricultural income and animal products 35·5 per cent. The volume of investment in agricultural projects was estimated at about JD 13 million, but actual expenditure exceeded the planned figure.

The Five-Year Plan (1976–80) has also laid great stress on the need to develop the agricultural sector. It puts forward the following goals: to increase agricultural income from JD 30 million in 1975 to JD 42 million in 1980, i.e., an increase of 40 per cent or an average of 7·0 per cent per annum; and to increase the relative contribution of output towards meeting local consumption of essential agricultural commodities.

To achieve this, the government has formulated projects totalling JD 40 million. The Plan urges further development of the Jordan Valley, which is Jordan's most important agricultural area.

The Jordan Valley

The Jordan Valley is a rift valley 100 kilometres long and five to ten kilometres wide, running in a north–south direction between Lake Tiberias, which is 200 metres below sea level, and the Dead Sea, 400 metres below sea level. The valley is the nation's greenhouse. It has rich soil and is blessed with a climate conducive to year-round agricultural production. Total arable land in the East Jordan Valley is 360 000 dunums (90 000 acres). The potential of this huge natural farm is enormous. Given sufficient water it is capable of producing up to four crops a year. However, current agricultural production, farmers' incomes, social facilities and general living conditions leave much to be desired.

During the late 1950s and 1960s Jordan Valley development projects were concerned with improving agriculture; little was done to provide housing or social services for the farmers. Between 1967 and 1971 extensive fighting devastated most of the original valley settlements and drove the people to seek safety on the highland plateau.

Gradually the farmers returned, and now more than 70 000 people are living in nearly sixty diverse areas. Growth was haphazard even in the best of these communities, and nearly all lacked basic utilities and services. Most houses were poorly constructed of mud bricks. There was only one doctor resident in the valley; clinical facilities were inadequate, schools frequently makeshift, buildings overcrowded, and most water for domestic use was taken from polluted sources.

A regional development programme is now under way in the East Jordan Valley which is bringing about major physical, social and economic changes. This

The East Ghor Canal, centrepiece of the Jordan irrigation system

programme is gradually improving the quantity and quality of agricultural production, reducing the foreign trade deficit in agricultural commodities, and raising the living standards of the valley people.

To accomplish these changes the Jordan Valley Commission was created in 1973. The commission prepared the Jordan Valley Development Plan–an integrated rural-urban, physical, economic and social plan for regional agricultural development. The major objectives of the plan are to develop the land, water and human resources of the valley to their full potential, and so to increase agricultural production and curtail rural-urban migration.

The main agricultural floor of the rift valley, known as the Ghor, varies in width from two to six kilometres, and extends to the steep slopes which flank the eastern edge of the valley and rise 1000 metres to the highland plateau. The small transitional zone where the East Ghor agricultural land meets the valley slopes is the corridor area where new communities, urban services, and the main irrigation canal are being located. The Jordan River, which meanders south from Lake Tiberias in a narrow channel, has eroded the Ghor to form an extremely fertile flood plain–the Zor. The boundaries of the Zor are formed by unstable and saline slopes called Katar, leading up to the main Ghor valley floor.

Water is essential to the plan. Unfortunately the fame of the Jordan River is not matched by the quantity or quality of its water. It is a brackish stream, impossible for intensive irrigation. Water resources for irrigating the Ghor and Zor agricultural lands are available from tributaries flowing from the eastern highlands into the Jordan River. The Yarmouk River in the north and Zarqa River in the centre of the valley are the largest. Since 1963 the centrepiece of the irrigation system has been the East Ghor Canal, which draws most of its water from a diversion of the Yarmouk River.

Three reservoirs have been built on smaller tributaries of the Jordan: Ziqlab, 4 500 000 cubic metres capacity; Shueib, 2 300 000, and Kafrein, 4 300 000; these also supply water to the valley irrigation system. A major reservoir project, the King Talal Dam, has been completed on the Zarqa River. With a 52 000 000 cubic metres storage capacity, it channels water to the East Ghor Canal, and also enables 6300 hectares of land lying generally above the main canal to be sprinkler-irrigated. When completed the Yarmouk River Maqarin Dam project will provide water to sprinkler-irrigate an additional 15 000 hectares by extending the East Ghor Canal to the Dead Sea.

The most important component in development of the valley is the farming population. Attracting a larger population presents two problems. The small farmer must have sufficient land to form an economically viable farm unit, and basic urban services must be provided in a rural environment. The future economic viability of farms has been assured by a three-phase plan.

First is the construction of the East Ghor Canal irrigation programme, already two-thirds completed, which enables three or four crops to be raised yearly. The cost is amortized over the life of the project, thus reducing the initial cost of water to the farmers.

Second is the implementation of a realistic land reform programme, carried out in conjunction with irrigation construction; this allows present landowners to retain up to 200 dunums of land, and allocates 40–50 dunum agricultural units to formerly landless tenant farmers.

Third is the provision of agriculture-related support services. A farmers' association was organized to provide the farmer with credit facilities and easier access to all production inputs, seed, fertilizer, machinery and so on. The association is developing four grading and packing centres which will market the farmers' produce and increase their income by eliminating the need for middlemen.

The problem of providing urban services to a rural agricultural area is most difficult to solve economically. During the planning process, five basic regional planning principles were established: to use all potential irrigable agricultural land for farming; to allocate population growth within the valley on the basis of providing the necessary agricultural work forces; to locate villages only on land unsuitable for agricultural purposes and within three to four kilometres (walking distance) from farm land; to avoid areas with major physical problems, including large wadis, flood plains, erosion areas, sink holes, rock outcrops and areas of excessive slope; and to minimize the disturbance of the existing population, and protect investment, by retaining houses and facilities wherever feasible.

To facilitate the field plan, roads, pathways, residential lots, and all other urban land uses are designed within the framework of a six-metre-square grid. Highways are located in accordance with the East Ghor regional transport plan. The housing areas within villages are based on neighbourhood clusters of lots served by paved roads at a maximum of 100 metres distance. Full development of each planned community, however, is impeded by the prospective residents' lack of capital to provide their own housing. A possible means of solving the problem would be a price subsidy on the first residential lot. Sales of additional lots to wealthier inhabitants would be at market value.

Essential urban services, including domestic water, electricity, telecommunications and transport, are provided within the service corridor that runs the length of the Jordan Valley. Government and local municipal administrative services are grouped together within each settlement near the commercial centre. Regional government facilities, including courts, national ministries and licensing, are located in three administrative centres along the valley.

Within each village every neighbourhood has a separate boys' and girls' elementary and preparatory school. The secondary school system is divided into nine districts, each serving approximately equal populations. Their sites are located to allow easy access and minimize travel distances. In keeping with the development plan's emphasis on improving the quality of life, the school programme includes subjects usually found only in urban areas, physics and chemistry laboratories, home economics and good libraries.

The regional health service is divided into five districts based on population size and siting. Within each health service district is a medical centre to be staffed by two doctors, with emergency beds, X-ray units, laboratories and limited surgery facilities. Small outpatient health clinics with a visiting doctor are located near the centre of each village community.

Existing mosques, tombs and other religious sites have been preserved and, where possible, upgraded and incorporated into the villages as religious, cultural and recreational focal points. Local recreation areas are the school playgrounds and playing fields. Land unsuitable for building, such as wadis, rock outcrops, katar land and steep slopes, is to be converted into public open spaces or community pathways by tree planting, erosion control, or other appropriate measures.

By integrating the development of land, water and human resources, the Jordan Valley Commission aims at transforming the valley into one of the world's most intensively developed agricultural areas. Work opportunities created will help to slow the drift from rural to urban centres, ensure a better future for the valley farming community, and have a lasting impact on Jordan's economic and social development.

Trade and the Balance of Payments

External trade plays an important part in Jordan's economy. In the years 1973–5, commodity imports represented on average 35 per cent of the Gross National Product (GNP), and had to be relied upon to meet about one-fifth of total consumption. They provided more than one-third of the raw materials and intermediate goods needed for local industry, and contributed over a quarter of the nation's total fixed capital formation. On the other hand, commodity exports– about half of which were agricultural products – only constituted 10 per cent of the GNP; phosphate rock alone accounted for more than half the non-agricultural exports.

The average per capita share of foreign trade in Jordan increased from JD 39 in 1966 to JD 85 in 1975.

Jordan continues to depend on imports to a large extent to sustain production and maintain living standards. Like most developing nations, it continues to face a serious deficit in its external trade balance. Even when Jordan's present stage of development and the possibilities of its available natural resources are taken into consideration, the fact remains that the trade gap has persisted.

Hence, in formulating its national development policy, the government of Jordan decided that the rate at which the trade deficit was increasing had to be reduced. The Three-Year Development Plan (1973-75) acknowledged that the implementation of development projects, which depended on imported capital, goods and raw materials, would necessarily result in an increase in imports. But, at the same time, the Plan visualised that commodity exports would also increase at a rate that would restrain the growth of the trade deficit.

The first Five-Year Plan (1976-80) did not reverse the trend, and the second Five-Year Plan (1981-85) anticipates that the deficit will increase still further but that its ratio to the GNP will fall.

In the last two decades, Jordan has had an impressive expansion in its economy and momed a long way towards self-sufficiency. The ratio of commodity exports to commodity imports rose from 11 per cent in 1955 to 18 per cent in 1972, and the ratio of exports of goods and services to imports of goods and services rose from 27 per cent to 30 per cent in the same period.

The export and import figures since 1955 tell a story which, while leaving much to be desired, has some encouraging features. Exports (i.e. domestic exports and re-exports) increased from JD 2.9 million in 1955 to JD 4.0 million in 1960, JD 17.0 million in 1972, JD 50.0 million in 1975, and JD 120.9 million in 1979. This growth in commodity exports is largely due to considerable expansion in agricultural production and mineral extraction. Commodity imports, though, rose by about 58 per cent by 1960, were JD 68.2 million in 1966, over JD 95 million in 1972, JD 203 million in 1975, and JD 590 million, or thereabouts, in 1979. This sizable increase in imports has been largely due to the impressive economic growth throughout the period, with GNP increasing from JD 50 million in 1955 to JD 187 million in 1966, more than JD 252 million in 1972, more than JD 300 million in 1975, and more than JD 853 million in 1979. The growing need of the economy for intermediate and capital goods contributed significantly to this increase.

As a result, the gap between exports and imports has widened in absolute terms. The visible trade deficit increased by over 61 per cent between 1955 and 1960, and was about JD 271 million in 1976, and JD 468.6 million in 1979. While it is recognized that a trade gap of this magnitude constitutes a sizable claim on the country's economic resources, the level of the trade deficit as a proportion of the GNP decreased from about 48.6 per cent in 1955 to about 31 per cent in 1966 and 1972. It will be noted, however, that, owing to the importance of agriculture to economic activity and its heavy dependence on rainfall, this percentage rises in drought years and declines at other times. For example, the ratio of the trade deficit to GNP in 1971 – a year with adequate rainfall – was less than 28 per cent.

The composition of Jordan's exports underwent important changes in the period under review. Agricultural exports doubled in value between 1955 and 1963, were worth JD 5.5 million in 1972, JD 7 million in 1976, and over JD 21 million in 1979. This increase has been largely due to rapid expansion in exports of unprocessed agricultural commodities, mainly fruit and vegetables. These rose in value from JD 1.4 million in 1955 to JD 4.9 million in 1972.

With the completion of several agricultural development projects launched in the early sixties – particularly the East Ghor Canal scheme – Jordan has substantially expanded its agricultural production. The increase in production of fruit and vegetables has been sufficient to make the country self-sufficient in certain seasons, and able to supply neighbouring Arab countries to some extent as well. In spite of this, and as a result of the increase in the exportation of other products, agricultural exports in relation to total exports fell from 59 per cent in 1955 to 51 per cent

High-speed phosphates loading bay at Aqaba docks

in 1966, 43 per cent in 1972, and 25 per cent in 1979.

It is worth noting here that agricultural exports have consisted predominantly of unprocessed products, because agricultural processing industries have not been developed fully yet, and existing facilities cater primarily for domestic rather than outside markets.

The second most important item in Jordan's export trade is the phosphate industry. Whereas the position in the early fifties – both in absolute value and relative importance – was that phosphate was insignificant, extraction has increased remarkably, and phosphate has become the highest single foreign exchange earning commodity. Phosphate exports rose from about 21 per cent of domestic exports in 1955 to about 37 per cent in 1960. In the period 1968-72, they averaged around 28 per cent of total exports. They rose to 44 per cent of exports in 1976, and fell to about 31 per cent in 1979.

The export of manufactured commodities increased from JD 0.3 million in 1960 to JD 1.2 million in 1966, JD 3.6 million in 1972, to JD 33.3 million in 1979.

Exports of manufactured goods are varied and include cement, cigarettes, pharmaceuticals, paper and paper board, batteries and textiles. In proportion to total exports they rose from about 9 per cent in 1960 to about 15 per cent in 1966, 28.6 per cent in 1972, dropping slightly to about 27 per cent in 1979.

The importance of imports in Jordan's economy has already been noted. They are depended upon not only for consumption but also to provide the capital goods

Wool mill interior
Above left: Cement
plant in Fukais
Left: Batteries for
export

needed for development. Consumer goods constitute the biggest single item by value among Jordan's imports. According to the Department of Statistics, imports of consumer goods amounted to JD 20.5 million in 1955, rising to JD 42.2 million in 1966. After the 1967 war, the value of imported consumer goods fell to JD 29.4 million in 1968, then rose again to JD 57.7 million in 1972, reaching JD 200 million or more in 1979. Foodstuffs and beverages topped the list of imported consumer goods, with textiles and clothing coming next in importance.

In spite of the impressive agricultural and industrial development and the establishment of a number of import-replacing industries, the ratio of imports of consumer goods to total consumption expenditure continues to be high. This ratio has fluctuated from one year to another, rising in drought years, during which imports of foodstuffs – particularly wheat and wheat flour – naturally increased. Moreover, imports of durable consumer goods, owing to the rise in personal incomes, are becoming increasingly important; their value has risen year after year. With further development of the economy, Jordan will tend to become less dependent on imports of food and clothes, but should become, in the absence of well-developed local production, increasingly dependent on imports of durable consumer goods.

The second most important item among Jordan's imports is raw materials and intermediate commodities. Owing to the growing needs of local economic activity, imports of these commodities increased in value from JD 3.9 million in 1955 to nearly JD 180 million in 1979. Relative to total imports, they rose from 14 per cent in 1955 to about 31 per cent in 1966, then fell to about 30 per cent in 1972 and 1979.

Capital goods come third in importance. They increased in value from JD 2.6 million in 1955 to JD 9.6 million in 1972, fluctuating from one year to another, then rising steeply to JD 193.6 million in 1979.

The main outlet for Jordan's exports is in the Arab countries. Exports to these countries amounted to JD 9.2 million (73 per cent of total domestic exports) in 1972 and JD 56 million in 1979 as compared with JD 5.6 million in 1966. During this period, exports to the Arab Common Market (ACM) countries – Syria, Egypt, Iraq and the Sudan – increased strongly from about JD 1.2 million in 1955 to JD 30.3 million in 1979. Also significant, exports to other Arab countries – particularly Lebanon, Kuwait and Saudi Arabia, which are not members of the ACM – increased enormously, from JD 0.8 million in 1955 to JD 5.6 million in 1972 and more than JD 20 million in 1979.

India, Japan and Yugoslavia come next on Jordan's list of export outlets. Exports to these countries – almost entirely phosphate rock – increased from JD 0.3 million in 1955 to JD 2.5 million in 1969, fell to JD 2.2 million in 1972, then rose again to nearly JD 10 million in 1979.

As one of the five founding members of the Council for Arab Economic Unity and the Arab Common Market, Jordan is making a serious effort to find new markets for its products. Several bilateral trade agreements have been concluded with Arab and other countries.

Because of the structure and development pattern of the economy, Jordan's imports have come mostly from the developed countries. The European Economic Community, the United States and Japan supplied over half the Country's imports in the period 1969-72, while imports from the Arab countries comprised about 20 per cent of the total in that period, and up to 1979.

Saudi Arabia is the single most important source of imports for Jordan, followed by West Germany, then the United Kingdom, with the United States, Italy, Japan and France coming next in order of importance. The value of Jordan's imports from Saudi Arabia was JD 34 million in 1976, and JD 69 million in 1979. Imports from West Germany rose from a value of JD 52 million in 1976 to JD 68 million in 1979. Imports from the United Kingdom amounted to JD 24 million in 1976 and to JD 45 million in 1979. In the same period, imports from the United States rose from JD 31 million to JD 44 million. Purchases from the socialist countries (China, USSR, East Germany, Rumania, Poland, Bulgaria, Hungary and Czechoslovakia) have risen from JD 5.6 million in 1964 to JD 51 million in 1979.

As shown above, Jordan has always imported more goods than it has exported.

Inside the Jordan
Arab Bank, Amman

Because imports have risen faster than exports in absolute terms, the country has faced a growing trade deficit. This deficit has been partially covered by net earnings from invisible transactions and partially by unilateral private and official transfers.

The two most important elements in Jordan's invisible earnings are income from tourism and remittances from Jordanians living abroad.

The country is richly endowed with archaeological and religious sites, which have attracted increasing numbers of tourists from all over the world. In 1955 the number of tourists that came to Jordan was 85,000. In 1966, it was 620,000. The June 1967 War affected tourism drastically. In one week, Jordan lost its most important Holy Land sites – Jerusalem, Bethlehem, Hebron, Jericho – and a vital part of its land. Along with them went most of the country's tourist facilities. Consequently, income from tourism fell from JD 11.3 million in 1966 to JD 4.6 million in 1968. It climbed again to JD 8.3 million in 1972, JD 21 million in 1975, and an estimated JD 100 million in 1979.

The government of Jordan fully appreciates the tremendous importance of the tourist industry and the contribution it could make to economic growth. The Three-Year Plan (1973-75) recognized the need to develop resources on the East Bank, and gave high priority to projects that would increase the number of visitors and the length of their stay. The plan allowed for a total investment of JD 7 million in tourist facilities, and expected an increase of 150 per cent in income from this source between 1972 and 1975.

The Three-Year Plan had its effect. The number of non-Jordanian arrivals increased from 308,000 in 1973 to 552,704 in 1975, just over 1 million in 1976, and more than 1.6 million in 1980. This increase in the number of visitors has meant a growing demand for hotel accommodation, and hotels with a total capacity of 2300 rooms were built between 1977 and 1979. More have been constructed since.

Remittances account for quite substantial revenue. Within the last twenty years,

Jordan has been an exporter of skills and learning to the neighbouring Arab states and to some European countries. Thousands of Jordanians took up employment in these countries at comparatively attractive wages and remitted part of their earnings to their families at home. These amounted to JD 4.6 million in 1959 and JD 10.6 million in 1966. Following the June 1967 war, the amount of private transfers dropped to JD 4.1 million in 1968, then rose to JD 7.4 million in 1972, JD 180 million in 1979, and JD 236 million in 1980.

Jordan also receives official transfers of funds from other countries. The circumstances of Jordan's origin and subsequent development have necessitated heavy dependence on foreign aid, including financial support for government expenditure. In the years 1955-66, budget support and economic and technical assistance totalled JD 212.2 million, of which 71 per cent was received from the United States, 14 per cent from Arab countries and 13 per cent from Great Britain. In 1968, the central government received JD 40.1 million, of which JD 39.6 million was in the form of budget support and only JD 0.5 million in the form of economic and technical assistance. Provisional estimates for 1979 show a total in budget support of JD 213.2 million, with JD 9.0 million coming from the United States and JD 204.2 million coming from the Arab countries. There were no receipts of economic or technical assistance in 1979, but development loans totalling JD 39.3 million were received, mostly from Kuwait. In 1980, according to provisional estimates, the pattern was the same, with total budget support standing at JD 214.9 million, of which JD 6.1 million came from the United States and JD 208.8 million from the Arab countries. No economic or technical assistance was received in 1980, and development loans were in the order of JD 42.6 million, again mostly from Kuwait. The Western nations were replaced by Arab suppliers of budget support after the 1967 war. The United States resumed support in 1971, but is now only a minor participant.

Estimates of Jordan's balance of payments are published both annually and quarterly. They provide a summary of the most important transactions with other countries. These transactions fall into two main groups: Current Account, and Capital and Monetary Gold. The Current Account is composed of: (a) the balance of visible trade, that is, the difference between commodity imports and exports and re-exports; (b) the balance of invisibles, that is, services; and (c) net transfer payments. The second main group consists of the change in the assets of the non-monetary sector, that is, the private sector, local government and central government, in addition to the assets of the monetary sector, which comprises the central monetary institutions and commercial banks.

Because commodity imports have increasingly exceeded exports, the visible trade deficit rose from JD 21.7 million in 1955 to JD 77.9 million in 1972, and to JD 467 million in 1979. Though the balance of invisibles was positive in most of the years under review and helped to offset the imbalance in visible transactions, the country has continued to suffer from a negative balance of goods and services. The deficit rose from JD 16.0 million in 1955 to JD 35.6 million in 1966, and to JD 71.0 million in 1972, and JD 317 million in 1979.

Trade deficits of such magnitude could not have been sustained all these years had it not been for substantial injections of transfer payments. Net transfer payments rose from JD 15.8 million in 1955 to JD 34.1 million in 1966, JD 68.3 million in 1972 and JD 314.4 million in 1979. Moreover they have turned sizable

Jordan's highly sophisticated satellite communications station at Baqa'a
Left: King Hussein chats with a radio ham in Kuwait from the radio amateurs' centre in Madaba. Informal contacts with the outside world are encouraged

trade deficits into surpluses on current accounts in some of the years under review, and into manageable deficits on current accounts in the other years.

The balance on long-term capital accounts shows a consistent net inflow of capital into the country amounting to JD 2.5 million in 1955, JD 1.9 million in 1960. JD 5.2 million in 1966, JD 9.2 million in 1972, and more than JD 58 million in 1979.

Thus it has been possible for Jordan to achieve rapid economic growth, to meet all its financial obligations to the outside world, and to maintain internal and external economic stability.

Communications

The Telecommunications Corporation of Jordan (TCC) has prepared a long term telecommunication "Fundamental Plan" which had defined in detail the various telecommunication requirements for Jordan up to 1985 and has established the general framework for the requirements in this sector up to year 1995.

Based on this "Plan", TCC has decided to adopt the latest technology in electronic switching for its exchanges. Six electronic exchanges type Fetex – 100 were installed in Jordan each with a maximum capacity ranging between 20,000 - 30,000 lines. Four (4) of these exchanges were installed in the city of Amman, one in Irbid and the other in Karak. Those exchanges provided initially 31,000 lines and were put in service by the end of 1979. Seven other small electronic exchanges type "Pentex" each with a capacity of 1000 lines were installed in Amman (two exchanges), Mafraq, Ramtha, Jerash, Ma'an and Wadi Musa.

TCC has also completed expansion and upgrading works of the old electrome-chanical exchanges in Amman, Zarqa, Salt and Aqaba where 9,000 additional lines were provided.

In the field of local networks, TCC awarded a large contract for expansion and upgrading of the Amman local network and actual implementation of the project started by middle of 1980.

The following table shows the growth of available telephone lines in the main towns of Jordan:

TABLE I

	1975	1980
Amman	31,000	52,000
Zerqa	1,940	6,000
Irbid	2,000	9,000
Ramtha	400	1,000
Salt	1,200	3,000
Kerak	600	2,000
Ma'an	300	1,000
Aqaba	1,000	3,000

Telex Services had a major development programme where all the electrome-chanical exchanges in Amman, Irbid, Aqaba and Zerqa with an overall capacity of 890 lines were replaced by a centralized electronic exchange in Amman to serve the whole country. This exchange was initially equipped with 2032 lines.

A second Satellite Earth Station was installed and commissioned in August, 1979 at the Baqa'a complex. The new station, which was equipped with a larger capacity of circuits for telephone, telex and TV services, replaced the first station which was operating with the Atlantic Satellite. The Original Station was readjusted to operate with the Indian Satellite and was put into service in January 1980 and access to almost all countries of the world was then available.

A major regional telecommunication project was commissioned by installing a microwave link between Amman and Damascus with a capacity of 960 channels and a TV link.

A coaxial cable link was constructed between Sweileh and Amman to provide an alternative route for the microwave National and International networks.

National Direct Dialling between Amman, Zerqa and Irbid was expanded and the towns of Aqaba and Salt were added to the Direct Dialling Network.

In May 1979 a contract was signed for providing a fully electronic national and international digital exchange type MT 20, and is expected to be commissioned during 1982. This exchange will provide automatic direct dialling telephone services both nationally and internationally.

A total investment of about 28 million JD was spent on projects implemented during the Five Year Plan period of 1976-1980.

In the administration and organization fields, TCC has recruited qualified international consultancy services to prepare man-power training and development programmes for administrative and technical staff. A new organization structure was adopted including the establishment of a commercial section within the Finance Department and the first commercial budget and operating accounts were prepared for the years 1978 and 1979. This showed a substantial growth in assets, re-

venue and operating costs as follows:
(Million JD's)

	1977	1978	1979
Net - Assets	12.5	15.5	16.4
Annual Revenue	-	6.7	8.1
Operating Costs	-	3.7	5.2

Training activities were intensified for the various specialties of telecommunications through the training centre in Amman and through scholarships abroad for a large number of engineers and technicians, on site training was provided by manufacturers experts on projects.

The Goals

1. To upgrade the quality and efficiency of Telecommunication services and provide for adequate services to meet the continuous demand.
2. To provide financial coverage of all operating costs and secure adequate saving to finance new projects and debt services.
3. To increase the telephone penetration ratio in the various towns and villages to meet with the urgent demand as follows:

TABLE II
No. of telephones for 100 population

	1980	1985
Amman	5.0	20
Irbid	7.8	12
Zerqa	2.8	10
Aqaba	10.4	20
Salt	9.1	12
Ramtha	3.7	10
Mafraq	4.6	7
Jerash	9.8	14
Ma'an	8.8	12
Kerak	16.9	17
Madaba	2.0	10
Large Villages	3.0	10
Medium Villages	2.0	7
Small Villages	1.0	5

4. Provide an even and balanced geographical distribution of telephone services in the country to cover most of the rural areas of Jordan and provide services for every population centre with more than 500 people which includes about 370 towns and villages.
5. Provide community telephone services for about 50% of the small population centres with less than 500 people. This will include about 360 centres.
6. Provide for fully automatic national and international telephone direct dialling through international exchanges, earth stations and regional and national toll networks.
7. Expansion of telex services to be able to meet all of the demand in any town of Jordan.
8. The automatization of telegraph services and introduction of Pentex through the electronic telex exchange in Amman.

In the wake of the 1967 war, displaced Palestinians camp on the edge of the Jordanian desert. International aid has helped fund their rehabilitation

Welfare

Jordan's social structure, its organization and its welfare services are rooted in the values and traditions of Arab Muslim culture. One of the five basic pillars of faith in Islam is the practice of alms-giving and care of the needy. Today in Jordan this has become a blend of ancient religious obligation and modern concepts of civic consciousness and governmental concern.

The implementation of the social welfare programme is a partnership between the State and voluntary agencies. This partnership has been happy and fruitful; and because Jordan is one of the smallest countries in the area and its people form a rather large family, some impressive results have been achieved which have placed the Hashemite Kingdom in a leading position in this field.

The chain of events accompanying the development of social welfare in Jordan has been dramatic. It started with the arrival of about half a million refugees in 1948, and continued with a fresh influx of about 250 000 persons, displaced in 1967 as a result of the third Arab–Israeli war. All this put the country's welfare services under great strain, and made the need for assistance imperative. Friendly religious, philanthropic and international organizations gave help; some still do so. At the same time, the State reinforced the existing measures and continued to develop the country's services.

It has been the practice in Jordan to co-ordinate state activities with those of the local and foreign voluntary agencies to meet local needs. This policy is bearing fruit at the moment and should continue to do so in the future.

The main objectives of social welfare in Jordan are embodied in Law Number 14 of the Ministry of Labour and Social Affairs, enacted in 1956. This law provides for social security, self help and the co-ordination of social services among all age groups. It defines the scope of social welfare under the following headings:

1. Providing assistance to individuals, families, co-operatives, social societies, labour syndicates and other agencies and institutions engaged in welfare work.
2. Supporting institutions carrying out objectives of the Ministry of Labour and Social Affairs such as homes for illegitimate infants, homeless children and mentally retarded persons; homes for the aged, orphans and juvenile delinquents; centres for the rehabilitation of boys and girls, and probationary or reformatory agencies and vocational training centres.
3. Developing small communities, including the encouragement of cottage industries and handicrafts, the construction of public parks, the improvement of local administration and the raising of standards of living in general.
4. Promoting sports, educational, artistic and scouting movements, establishing sports and cultural clubs and adult literacy centres.
5. Preparing recreational programmes for male and female students during summer vacations.
6. Solving problems of homelessness, street begging, prostitution and the exploitation of children and women, and organizing a welfare police service.
7. Supervising recreational places such as nightclubs, cinemas and theatres, and the censorship of films, plays and floor shows.
8. Guiding youth and controlling juvenile delinquents, and providing care and jobs for them after serving their sentence.
9. Providing family and child care.
10. Supervising labour affairs and the registration of employers' associations, trade unions, and areas such as workmen's compensation and rewards, health and safety regulations, industrial safety and the improvement of working conditions, insurance and social security, vocational training, protection of the young and control of foreign labour.
11. Dealing with housing problems and encouraging the construction of low cost homes.
12. Carrying out social research, collecting and publishing social statistics, and providing grants for such purposes.

Social welfare agencies fall into two main categories, state and voluntary. The state agencies include the ministries of Labour and Social Affairs, Education, Health, Municipal and Rural Affairs, the Interior, and Religious and Islamic Affairs, as well as the Youth and Sports Organization, the Co-operative Organization and the Housing Corporation. The voluntary agencies include the Union of Charitable Societies, the Red Crescent Society, the Anti-Tuberculosis Association, and the foreign voluntary societies.

The Ministry of Labour and Social Affairs is mainly concerned with initiating and implementing all kinds of social development projects. It supervises and co-ordinates the activities of all agencies in this field, and is represented in all Governorates of the Kingdom. In addition to the services already listed, it extends material assistance to needy families, orphans, widows and victims of natural disasters or chronic diseases, and gives encouragement and assistance to vocational training centres and centres for training social workers. Attached to the ministry is the Jordan Institute of Social Work, which is the main agency for the provision of training for new social workers and of refresher courses for social workers already employed. The institute provides a two-year course for secondary school

Study in concentration. Class in the Musa Alami orphanage school

graduates, and also studies and researches into the different aspects of social work. So far 131 social workers have graduated since the institute was established.

Each of the other governmental agencies carries out a specialized role in the social field. The Ministry of Education supervises all educational work done by the voluntary agencies. It operates 221 centres for combating illiteracy, inspects the work done by over 200 kindergarten centres, and offers books and educational materials to all students in government schools, who constitute about 26 per cent of the total population of the country. The Ministry of Health supervises the health service activities of voluntary agencies, and offers medical services to the poor, over and above the national vaccination schemes. The Ministry of the Interior offers assistance in the field of juvenile delinquency, and social care and counselling for prisoners and convicts. The Ministry of Municipal and Rural Affairs constructs rural schools and clinics in co-operation with the people and the voluntary agencies. The Ministry of Islamic and Religious Affairs offers spiritual guidance, and cares for orphans, providing them with vocational training.

The Youth and Sports Organization is entrusted with the encouragement and propagation of youth activities, the instilling of artistic values, the development of the team spirit and the encouragement of self-dependence among Jordanian youth. It is the sole agency responsible for the study, evaluation, approval and registration of youth centres. Since its establishment in 1966, it has brought together and assisted about 60 different clubs for athletic, educational or cultural purposes. It has also established and organized 25 youth centres with a total membership of about 1000. It has organized and developed the scout movement, consisting of about 300 units, with a total membership of about 10 000. The organization also co-operates with the Ministry of Education in constructing playgrounds and training sports leaders. It also operates the Hussein Sports City, which contributes a great deal to the aims and objectives of the organization.

An important part of the work of social development is carried out by private agencies. Their representative body is the Central Union of Voluntary Welfare Societies, comprising five district unions on the East Bank of Jordan. It is the major means for stimulating greater awareness among the people of the need to help the poor to help themselves. It also enables member societies to conduct elections democratically and delegate responsibilities without regard to religion, colour or sex. Voluntary charitable work covers both rural and urban areas. In East Jordan there are 206 societies with a total membership of about 10 000. Member societies are engaged in one or more of the following activities: provision of material assistance for needy people, establishment and operation of food centres, child-care centres, homes for the aged, vocational training centres, schools, kindergartens, nurseries, maternity centres, social centres and religious education centres. The number of persons benefiting from their welfare and charitable activities is over 60 000.

The present Central Union was established in 1959, and since then has been providing co-ordination between societies, district unions and the respective ministries. The governing body of the union is its general assembly which elects its board of directors. The chairman of the general assembly is the Minister of Labour and Social Affairs.

The latest developments of the Central Union are the establishment of a marketing agency to help market the societies' products (handicrafts and needlework), and the establishment of the Jordan Welfare Lottery. Both agencies were created to increase the income of the union.

Among the major independent and specialist voluntary welfare agencies is the Jordan National Red Crescent Society. It was started in 1947, was recognized by the International Committee of the Red Cross in 1948 and became a member of the league of the International Red Cross in 1950. Membership is open to all citizens and no special qualifications are required. The society has twenty-three branches; each branch elects its local executive committee of ten which runs the affairs of the branch. Representatives of the branches make up the general assembly of the society which in turn elects the central executive committee.

The activities of JNRCS are more specialized than those of the Union of Welfare Societies, because they are more concerned with health and medical affairs. They include hospitals, where medical care is provided for needy people (each acts also as a maternity centre), mother and child care (a function of all branches), out-patient clinics where the needy receive treatment and free medicine, first aid training and food centres (which are also a main activity of all branches). The JNRCS also cares for retarded and incapacitated people, and provides relief for victims of natural disasters, fires and war.

Government agencies and a number of voluntary organizations provide free maternity and child health care

The National Anti-Tuberculosis Association is an active, specialist voluntary agency, started in 1958, which now offers its services with a great deal of vigour, experience and co-ordination. It started with a limited voluntary membership, and today has hundreds of members in branches that cover all districts of the country. The active character of the branches apparently stems from the fact that they enjoy independence while still attached to the main society. The association was first recognized by the International Union Against Tuberculosis, and then became a member of the union, which is an international federation promoting tuberculosis control.

The NATA is engaged in the preparation of information on the causes, treatment and prevention of tuberculosis, taking an active role in TB combat programmes, offering medical care and material assistance to tubercular patients, actively participating in scientific research in the field of TB and attending local, regional and international conferences. The association has achieved excellent results in its BCG vaccination programmes, laboratory sputum examinations and the chest X-rays carried out by its mobile X-ray unit. The association was able to help increase the number of sanitoria in the country to five and out-patient clinics to eight. TB tests number over 100 000 a year, as do BCG vaccinations.

The number of people received annually by the TB out-patient clinics is about 150 000, and the Anti-Tuberculosis Association enjoys close collaboration and co-operation with the Ministry of Health.

As yet Jordan's social security programme comes nowhere near covering the whole nation. It does, however, cover all civil servants and workers in industry. The development and growth of social security has kept pace with the development and growth of state resources and the Gross National Income.

The first social security enactment was the pension fund legislation which covered all civil servants and members of the armed forces. Under this legislation any classified civil servant receives on retirement a pension equivalent to his last basic salary multiplied by the total number of months served divided by 480, provided the employee has completed twenty years of service or more (15 years for women); while the non-classified employees, or classified employees who have not completed twenty years of service, are entitled to a service reward equivalent to a monthly salary for every year's service, provided the period of service is more than five years. The pension is usually for the lifetime of the employee and can be inherited only by his widow and unmarried daughters. All classified employees contribute about 7 per cent of their monthly salary to the retirement fund.

This act was followed in 1966 by another social security ordinance which established a contributary fund. Each state employee contributes to this fund an amount relative to his salary. The contributions consist of a maximum of 800 fils and a minimum of 200 fils monthly. In return, the fund offers the civil servants the following benefits. In the event of death during service or any incapacitating injury, the employee or his heirs will receive the sum of JD 300, plus JD 25 for every year of service completed, provided the total paid does not exceed JD 800. In the event of death of any member of the employee's family he is entitled to a grant of JD 50. On retirement, the civil servant receives a single payment from this fund, equalling three months' salary, including the usual allowances.

The Workmen's Compensation Scheme ensures that a worker receives compensation for any degree of incapacity. The compensation for death is equivalent to the total wages the workman earns in a thousand days' work. In these cases the compensation cannot be more than JD 550 or less than JD 450. The compensation for complete incapacity is the equivalent of the wages earned by the workman concerned in 1200 working days, provided the total does not exceed JD 700; it cannot be below JD 500. Any workman injured during or as a result of the work he is doing, provided the injury is curable, is entitled to half his wages until the cure is complete.

Within certain limits, the law provides for service rewards for workmen upon the termination of their services or their resignation. This law has undergone several amendments, the latest in 1972. The minimum period of work that entitles a worker to compensation is six months and the reward is half a month's salary. After four years of service the reward is half a month's salary for each year, and for longer periods it is a month's salary for every year's service.

Before 1972, the reward was a month's salary for each of the first three years of service, and half a month's salary for each of the years in the rest of the period, provided the total reward did not exceed nine months' salary. This made the maximum period of reward fifteen years' service. Accordingly, workmen who had more than ten years' service, and less than fifteen years, received two-thirds of the total reward, and those who had more than five years of service, but less than ten years received one-third of the total reward. This reward was additional to any benefits that the workman may have earned from a savings fund, or any other pension fund that his firm might have established.

The government has issued a new security law, which grants generous privileges to workmen. This law embodied the most up-to-date ideas of social security practised in modern societies.

In 1966, the Health Insurance Act was passed, establishing a fund to meet all the expenses of medical service for eligible persons. The legislation covers all civil servants and retired government employees whose total income is more than

JD 100 annually. Every member is expected to contribute JD 0·5 monthly in return for the services available from governmental clinics and hospitals. Beneficiaries and members of their families are entitled to receive complete medical service, including clinical diagnosis and advice, laboratory tests, X-rays, hospitalization and surgical operations. Membership of the fund is open to the public, but they contribute 30 per cent more than qualified members. Citizens who earn less than JD 100 annually are provided with health insurance free of charge.

Health

Jordan's health services and administration have developed steadily since the 1950s and today provide the most advanced medical care to be found in the Arab world. At government public health and preventive care centres throughout the country, Jordan's people receive free maternity and child health services, immunization, and general medical attention. The country boasts two of the finest and most modern hospitals in the Middle East and highly trained Jordanian doctors are to be found not only at home but in many other countries. The policy of state health services in parallel with a private medical sector has proved its worth, although with a rapidly growing population the needs and scope of health work are continually expanding.

The Ministry of Health came into existence as a Directorate of Health in the Ministry of the Interior. Its budget in 1939 did not exceed JD 11 000 and the number of physicians was no more than twenty. But the increase in Jordan's population necessitated expansion, especially in the department's technical and administrative staff. In 1950, the Directorate of Health became the first Ministry of Health as the country came to grips with both immediate rudimentary needs and long-term planning requirements. In 1951 the budget for health was JD 240 774. By 1981 it had increased to JD 30 million.

The ministry comprises the Supreme Health Council and a high planning committee composed of all the ministerial directors. The East Bank is divided into eight health directorates, namely Amman, Zarqa, Balqa'a, Irbid, Mafraq, Karak, Tafila and Ma'an. All provide full health services, including the necessary laboratory work. They also provide services in preventive as well as curative medicine, medicinals, dental services, nursing, health education and training and health insurance.

The ministry pays great attention to preventive medicine. It imposes strict rules and regulations concerning the control of infectious diseases in the Kingdom, and as a result these have decreased appreciably.

It is obligatory for newborn infants to be vaccinated or immunized against smallpox, tuberculosis, poliomyelitis, DPT and measles. The ministry also conducted mass vaccination campaigns against smallpox in 1961, 1962 and 1965; poliomyelitis in 1964 and 1976; typhoid in 1960 and 1962; and cholera in 1966, 1970 and 1976.

Malaria had been a hazard in Jordan since ancient times, especially in the steamy climate of the Jordan Valley. Starting in 1949 the Ministry of Health and its medical staff worked hard to stamp it out. Continuous epidemiological and entomological surveys have since helped keep malaria under control. The success of the eradica-

The 550-bed Jordan University Hospital offers service for a token fee. Jordan's doctors are highly trained, and provide the most advanced medical care to be found in the Arab world

tion programme was due to the advice of and close co-operation with experts from the World Health Organization (WHO), the United States Agency for International Development (USAID) and the United Nations Children's Fund (UNICEF).

The Environmental Health Division was started in 1952 with four public health projects: a sanitation survey for the municipality of Amman; sanitary equipment and supplies for the municipality of Amman; building a sewage treatment plant for the city of Salt; and the provision of a safe water supply system for the municipality of Ma'an. The activities of the division have expanded to cover municipal sanitation, food, hygiene, industrial hygiene, health education, training courses for sanitary inspectors, food handlers, school teachers and school children, and the control of communicable diseases.

The Mother and Child Health Centres (MCH) project was started by establishing a training and demonstration centre in Amman in 1955. WHO provided the experts and UNICEF helped and is still helping with equipment and transport as well as milk and food supplements. MCH covers ante-natal care, home delivery services, child welfare, vaccination, nutrient and food supplements, health education and home visits.

The School Health Division started in 1969/70, and has since expanded to

135

cover the whole country. The objectives and duties of the division are: regular medical supervision of schoolchildren and their environment; sound and effective health education in and through the schools; the prevention and control of communicable diseases in schools; medical supervision of school meals; inspection of school premises and the provision of safe and healthy environments; and training of teachers in health education.

The Jordan Vaccine Institute (JVI) was established in 1964 for the production and distribution of human vaccines under the supervision of WHO. The vaccines it prepares are anti-rabies, smallpox, DPT (triple vaccine), cholera, typhoid and the combined D & T. It also prepares Casoni, Tuberculin and Widal antigens. It imports and distributes poliomyelitis and yellow fever vaccines. The JVI exports vaccines regularly to Syria through UNICEF and to other countries in the region in cases of epidemics.

Tuberculosis is the main public health problem in Jordan. As more of the nomadic Bedouin settle in towns so the number of people vulnerable to the disease increases. TB is unknown in the normal Bedouin habitat and they therefore have no resistance to it. Active measures to combat and prevent the spread of TB were started in 1953 and the burden has been borne mainly by the government and to some extent by the Jordan Anti-Tuberculosis Association.

Progress in fighting TB up to 1976 is reflected in the following statistics. In 1953 there were two TB hospitals with 180 beds, two TB centres, 21 040 medical examinations, 63 389 tuberculin tests and the number of bacillus Calmette–Guerin (BCG) vaccinations was 15 102. In 1976 the number of hospitals was three, the number of centres 17, the number of medical examinations 392 806, tuberculin tests 124 044, and BCG vaccinations 611 419.

The National Anti-Tuberculosis Association co-operates closely with the Ministry of Health.

The ministry is endeavouring to complete the establishment of a referral laboratory for chest diseases, linked with microscopy units which are spread among laboratories throughout the country. Since 1952 the Chest Diseases Division has been sending out mobile teams to all parts of the country to conduct investigations and vaccinations.

The ministry's medical services are made available to the public through hospitals, clinics, X-ray laboratories, blood banks, and distribution of medicines. Government hospitals are the backbone of the service. In 1951 the number of hospitals was 10, with 623 beds. The number of admissions was 9563; of operations, 2876; and of delivery cases, 209. In 1976 there were 12 government hospitals on the East Bank, with 1360 beds, 62 619 admissions, 23 220 operations, and 11 473 delivery cases.

The Ministry of Health has opened clinics throughout the Kingdom. In 1951 there were 46 clinics and the number of attendances was 352 320, while in 1976 the number of clinics was 332 and attendances 2 209 328.

The Dental Department was established in 1966 with three dental offices. In 1967 there were 10 dental clinics and 32 505 attendances. In 1976 there were 28 clinics and 136 142 attendances. All dental clinics perform extractions, fillings, endodontic treatment, periodontal treatment, diagnosis with the aid of radiography, prosthetics, minor oral surgery and orthodontic treatment.

The Blood Bank of Amman started in 1957, and up to the end of April 1960

136

the number of donors had reached 2500, blood transfusions 12 500; grouping and RH tests numbered 1900. In 1976 the number of donors was 9130, blood transfusions 5886 and grouping and RH tests 117 067. A national committee was established to aid the nation-wide blood banks project.

The Radiology Division was established in 1951 in a small way. The number of radiographs that year was 316, while in 1976 the number of plain radiographs reached 146 854 and coloured ones 35 237. In 1958 a special division was established for the treatment of malignant diseases and tumours, and atomic therapy techniques with the use of the cobalt machine were introduced. In 1966 medical physics was introduced and in 1971 a division using radium and radiotherapy techniques was started.

The Department of Planning and Supplies is responsible for the control of imported and locally manufactured drugs through a technical committee which licenses pharmacies, drug stores and pharmaceutical manufacturers; controls imports and consumption of narcotics for medical purposes; purchases drugs and all medical and non-medical supplies; and supervises the storage and issue of medical and non-medical supplies.

Laboratories were first started in Jordan in 1927. Now each hospital has a laboratory for all routine examinations. There were 347 613 laboratory examinations in 1975. Central government laboratories carry out diagnostic examinations, chemical quality tests, and drug and food analysis. Examinations performed by these laboratories also include TB, serology, bacteriology, toxicology, and analytical chemistry.

A school of nursing was founded in 1953 and in 1966 was designated a college. It offers a three-year training programme in theoretical and practical subjects. In 1976, fifty-six male and female staff nurses graduated from the faculty.

The Midwifery School was established with the co-operation of UNICEF. The period of study is two years. In 1976 eight midwives graduated. The Karak Practical Nursing School was established in 1968, offering a one-month course including theory and practice. The number of graduates in 1976 was fourteen.

The Para-Medical Institute was established in 1973. It includes laboratories, pharmacy, X-ray, medical physics therapy, anaesthesia, health inspection, vital and medical statistics, and dental technology. The period of study is two years. The number of graduates in 1973 was 173.

The Ministry of Health has founded health centres in Ramtha, Irbid, Rabbeh, Karak, Northern Shuneh, Madaba and Amman. Each centre has sections covering minor surgery, gynaecology, health education, MCH, and polyclinics.

The pride of the Kingdom's sixty hospitals is the Hussein Medical Centre, a 700-bed military hospital with a large out-patients department. Situated on a 150-acre site in the suburbs of Amman, this multi-speciality hospital offers Jordanians and foreigners treatment not available elsewhere. Medical services in the armed forces, however, are not restricted to forces personnel, but are available to their families, and others, free of charge, whether in clinics or hospitals. These medical services cover approximately 400 000 people. The increase in attendance at clinics, admissions to hospitals for surgical operations, and the open-heart surgery and organ transplants performed at Al Hussein Medical Centre are evidence of the success of the Royal Medical Services.

The medical faculty of Jordan University is increasingly becoming the source

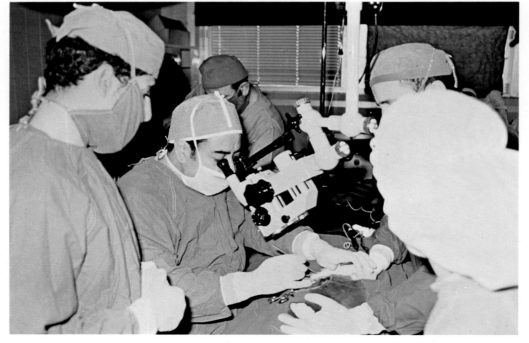

Pride of Jordan's sixty hospitals, the Hussein Medical Centre. In addition to the 700-bed general hospital which serves the armed forces, the complex encompasses the Princess Muna College of Nursing and living quarters for medical staff
Left: Operating theatre in the Hussein Medical Centre. Advanced surgical techniques, such as open-heart surgery, neuro-surgery, plastic surgery and maxilliary facial surgery, are placed at the disposal of Jordanians and foreigners alike

of home-trained physicians and surgeons, and the 550-bed University Hospital close to the campus is the country's teaching hospital. It was opened in 1973, as was the Hussein Medical Centre, which it complements. The University Hospital is equally well equipped and modern, but is planned on different lines. No ward contains more than six beds, and some wards can be used for single or double occupancy. The service is available for a token fee.

Health services offered by the Ministry of Municipal and Rural Affairs include inspection of restaurants and butcheries, surveillance of wells and sterilization of spring water with chlorine. There is close co-operation between the Ministry of Health and local government health departments.

After the events of 1948, the UN founded the United Nations Relief and Works Agency (UNRWA) to take care of refugees, especially in matters of health. UNRWA opened clinics and hospitals, and staffed them with doctors, dentists, pharmacists and nurses. It has signed an agreement with the Ministry of Health and the private sector by which a fixed number of beds are reserved for refugees in government and private hospitals.

Health and medical services are also available through semi-public hospitals, clinics, laboratories and radiography units. Foreign and national missions, too, run hospitals and clinics in Jordan. There are eight such hospitals on the East Bank with 383 beds, and 33 clinics where attendances reached 156 982 in 1976.

The extensive private sector offers health services, both preventive and curative, through hospitals, clinics, laboratories and pharmacies. It is very difficult to evaluate these services because they do not report to the Ministry of Health. This sector runs 19 hospitals in Amman with 440 beds.

12 Jordan for the Tourist

It comes as no surprise that tourism is one of Jordan's fastest growing industries. Scenically and historically the Hashemite Kingdom is rich in attractions for the traveller. Its traditions are the heritage of most of the civilized world, so that visiting Jordan becomes a kind of spiritual homecoming. In the hills west of the Jordan River, within the districts of Jerusalem and Nablus, stand hallowed shrines sacred to the world's monotheistic religions. On the East Bank are three internationally prized tourist sites—Petra, Wadi Rumm and Jerash, all conveniently accessible by road from Amman. The climate is good—hot in summer but dry, and cool at night except in Aqaba or the Dead Sea—and English is widely spoken as a second language.

We have seen something of what Jordan has to offer the tourist in the pages on the country's antiquities. But of course there is much more. Jordan has modern amenities as well as ancient glories.

The first thing you notice when the plane comes in to land is the colour of the country—terracotta slashed with vibrant green, the colours of mountains, buildings, forests and oases. Leaving the airport for the capital, you become aware of the clean, jasmine-scented air. Amman itself offers you the double pleasure of modern living, in a choice of hotels approved by the Ministry of Tourism, and the stimulus of a Middle Eastern environment where layer upon layer of history can be explored.

In Amman you can watch a play or listen to a concert in a Roman amphitheatre with perfect acoustics, restored to its original splendour by the Department of Antiquities. You can visit museums showing the folk arts of today or the treasures unearthed by archaeologists in dozens of historic sites. You can watch coal-black Arab stallions or haughty ill-tempered camels on the race course. You can sample traditional Arab dishes, with fruit fresh from the Jordan Valley. You will mingle with the colourful crowd, visit the shops in the *souks*, and hear the muezzin calling the faithful to prayer from his minaret in a chant that echoes across the hills.

There are souvenir shops with attractive native products at reasonable prices: necklaces, earrings and bracelets, hand-painted pottery and hand-blown glass, mother of pearl boxes, and Bibles and Korans in mother of pearl bindings, carved animals, chess pieces and nativity sets in attractively grained olive wood, modern and antique copper and brass ornaments and utensils, carpets and textiles, beautiful kaftans in cotton and rich velvets, some with gold and silver thread, Crusader jackets and Bedouin garments.

In addition you can enjoy the conventional pleasures of a tourist resort: cinemas with films from many countries, theatres, night clubs for wining, dining and dancing to resident bands, live music at some of the hotels, and colour television with an English-language channel.

Azraq Oasis, the only permanent body of water in 12 000 square miles of desert

141

Jordan has many efficient tourist agencies offering organized tours to suit all tastes. There is a network of very good roads linking Amman to virtually all the major tourist sites.

A forty-five-minute drive north of Amman takes you through the rolling hills of ancient Gilead to Jerash, the Roman city of Gerasa. In its columned streets you can visualize the legionaries on vacation and imagine the clatter of chariots on the paved roads. There is a modern rest-house at the site where you can have lunch and bring yourself back to the present.

Jerash was one of the rich Graeco-Roman cities of the Decapolis, a caravan station trading in precious stones, spices, silks, ivory and precious metals. When Rome declined, so did these cities, and earthquakes completed the work of centuries of decay. Jerash was not merely dead but forgotten, until, as recently as the 1920s, archaeologists saw columns protruding from the sand and unearthed this magnificent relic of former greatness. Much of the city has been restored to delight Jordanians and their guests alike.

If you have never seen an oasis, the pools of Azraq are well worth a visit. Eighty kilometres east of Amman the desert suddenly blossoms into eucalyptus, date palms and tamarisk. The pools are visited in spring and autumn by thousands of migrating birds. Hunting and hawking are the traditional sports of Azraq. Its marshes have been made into a National Wildlife Conservatory, and hunting is controlled by government licence during open season. Now an international biological station and a national park are being planned there.

It was here that Lawrence of Arabia wintered during the Arab Revolt, and planned his spectacular campaigns against the Turks. Azraq also has much older military associations. There is a Roman fortress built of monolithic slabs of basalt (lava rock) in AD 300, and inside it a mosque restored by Ezz Edin Aybak in the thirteenth century. Nearby are two villages built of basalt which stand, stark and beautiful, on the edge of the great lava desert which stretches as far as the eye can see.

From Azraq you can follow the wheel tracks across the desert to the famous Omayyad Desert Castles. Qasr Amra, built in the reign of Caliph Walid I in AD 710, was a palace of pleasure, with triple-roofed halls, frescoed siesta rooms and ornate steam baths. Very different is Qasr Al Kharana, an eighth-century fortress, its heavy stone walls pierced by arrow slits to protect the hunting stables of the square courtyard within. Its grimness is relieved by the carvings and frescoes in the walls of the upper chamber.

The ornate eighth-century castle of Qasr Al Mushatta was left uncompleted, its three eroded vaulted brick halls decorated with plaster carvings like stiff embroidery. Qasr Al Hallabat dates from about AD 200, when it was built by the Romans on an earlier, perhaps Nabataean, site. It was used as a monastery in the seventh century, a perfect place for solitude and meditation.

Driving due west from Jerash you come to the woods and mountains of Dibbeen, a national holiday resort. The road winds upwards through rich green countryside, where small villages and farms offer lettuces, melons and other produce for sale by the roadside. In Dibbeen National Park the government has built a restaurant and chalets amid the forests of Aleppo pines.

By the town of Ajloun you will come to a rare historic ruin. Qal'at Ar Rabad is one of the few castles surviving from Crusader times–with the difference that this

Jerash–the 'Pompeii of the Middle East'. Two centuries of lavish building converted Jerash from an inconspicuous village to a showplace of the Roman Empire, a city of vast colonnades, pagan temples, hippodromes and subterranean baths

143

was an Arab fortification built against, not by, the Crusaders. It stands on a hill from which, on a clear day, you can see across the Jordan Valley to Jerusalem.

Not far north is Irbid, one of the largest cities in Jordan, with hotels and restaurants for your refreshment and comfort. From here you can visit Umm Qeis to the north-west, standing on a hill overlooking Lake Tiberias and known as Gadara in biblical times. It was here that the Gadarene swine, possessed by evil spirits which Christ had cast out of men, flung themselves over the precipice. Villagers here are being rehoused so that the excavation and restoration of Gadara can continue.

South of Amman is Madaba, the first town on the historic King's Highway which follows the crest of the Mountains of Moab. Beautiful mosaic floors have been unearthed here, the most famous being in the Greek Orthodox Church of St George, which contains the astonishing sixth-century mosaic map of Jerusalem. The carpet weavers of Madaba reproduce some of the traditional mosaic patterns as well as more modern geometrical designs. When you have seen the treasures in Madaba's museum you can enjoy a meal in the government rest-house.

Ten kilometres north-west of Madaba, past villages where sheiks wear sheep-skin-lined robes and carry guns slotted into their belts, you arrive at Mount Nebo, most prominent point of the Moabite Range. From the top you have a magnificent view of the Dead Sea curving below you, the meandering river Jordan, and beyond a panorama of mountains. On a clear day, the crowning heights of Jerusalem are visible in the distance. At Syagha, on the summit of Nebo, Moses is said to have looked over the Jordan to the land of Canaan, and struck the rock at a spot now known as the spring of Ain Musa.

A road runs down from Mount Nebo to the bubbling hot mineral springs of Zarqa Ma'in where once King Herod bathed. The waters are as potent in mineral content as those of Baden-Baden and Wiesbaden in Germany. Close to the springs is Mukawir, where Herod's palace was situated and Salome danced before him. You can look across the rift valley to the Qumran caves.

From this point the road descends far below sea level to the briny shores of the Dead Sea, the earth's lowest body of water. The sea is indeed dead, for it is so dense with salts that no animal life can exist in its waters. One peculiar consequence of this property is that one cannot sink. The wader finds that when the water reaches his armpits he is swept off his feet, and when swimming his shoulders are always out of the water. There are numerous cafés along the shore and beach chalets and picnic areas are being built.

Further south along the King's Highway, on a ridge of the Moab Mountains where distances are still marked by the original Roman milestones, you come to the massive Crusader walls of Karak or 'Krac des Moabites'. From here the lord of Karak, Renaud de Châtillon, made his sorties against the Muslim caravans, until his capture and execution by Salah Al Din in 1187. The ruins still give a good idea of life in those violent medieval times. There is a village built within the battlements and a government rest-house nearby.

At Mu'tah and Mazar near Karak a great battle took place in AD 629 which was won by the forces of Islam. Here at dawn, say the local people, you can hear the noise of the battle carried on the air. Further south yet, the Crusader castle of Shobak stands majestically on a mountain peak; it is aptly named Monte Reale, 'Royal Mountain'.

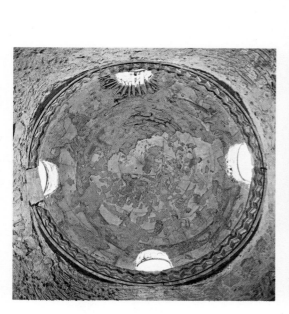

Frescoes on the dome of Qasr Amra, best
preserved of the Desert Castles
Above right : Qasr Amra, hunting lodge, baths
and 'pleasure dome' of the Omayyad caliphs
Right : The wooded highlands of Dibbeen
National Park

Mineral springs at Zarqa Ma'in, the Callirhoe of Herod's day

The most spectacular of Jordan's archaeological treasures is undoubtedly Petra, described already in these pages. To come across it suddenly, through the gloomy rock cleft (the Siq), is an experience never to be forgotten. It has been called a 'rose-red city', but in fact the rock out of which it has been hewn is many-coloured –violet, yellow and terracotta as well as the legendary pink.

From this tribal stronghold the Nabataeans, in around 300 BC, both protected and despoiled the passing caravans. Roman legions tried in vain to penetrate the Siq, till they discovered and cut the conduit from Wadi Musa which brought water to the inhabitants. Houses, temples, tombs and palaces are carved deep into the rock. A flight of 1045 steps leads up to the High Place, where stood the altar of the Nabataean god Dushara, and from which troughs carried off the blood of sacrifice.

If you want to spend some time exploring this mysterious city, in which the Queen of Sheba stayed and which Cleopatra possessed briefly, you can put up at the excellent government rest-house situated just outside the Siq. It occupies the site of the customs shed, where fees were 'collected' from passing caravans. Inside Petra itself there is a small hotel and a camp site and, for the hardy, sleeping accommodation in some of the caves and tombs. Accommodation can also be had in the green village of Wadi Musa nearby.

Visitors are warned that the sale of antiquities is now prohibited in Jordan, but many of the objects offered by the Bedouin at Petra are good copies.

From Petra, one of the most dramatic drives in the world lies south, dropping from the mountain plateau at Ras En Naqb to the eerie valley of Wadi Rumm. Two miles wide and twelve long, this magnificent lunar landscape of pink sands and black mountains, shimmering with mirages, will be remembered from the

146

Karak or 'Krac des Moabites', most imposing of the Crusader castles, dominates the Dead Sea a thousand metres below
Right: Petra, 'rose-red city half as old as time'. Chiseled from the mountainside with a sublime indifference to scale, the immense monument known as the *Khazneh* (or Treasury) stands entire, as if the Nabataeans had quietly departed only yesterday

Dawn reveals a
Bedouin encampment
at Qa'al Disi

film *Lawrence of Arabia*. Here the two-towered fort of the mounted police of the Desert Camel Corps stands small and defiant. Here water from 'Lawrence's Wells' flows perennially down copper-veined cliffs; here Bedouin flocks come to drink. From this spot, sparsely inhabited by herdsmen who live in black goatskin tents, you can hire camels and trek for several days in the desert accompanied by a guide.

At Qa'al Disi, at the end of Wadi Rumm, is an experimental agricultural station, where the desert comes to life with barley and wheat fields. A wonderful sight is the desert after a rare rainfall, when it bursts into flower for an all too brief spell.

The King's Highway ends at Aqaba, five hours by road and one hour by air from Amman. Backed by purple mountains, fringed by palms, Aqaba is Jordan's only port and seaside resort, a commercial lifeline and playground in one. To the tourist it offers all the pleasures of sand, sea and continuous sunshine. Its crystal waters provide every sort of sport for the strenuous, and at a gentler pace there are cruises in glass-bottomed boats for viewing the enchanting underwater life of the coral reefs. There are excellent hotels with adjacent chalets, all air conditioned, and a choice of good restaurants. There are bars and discotheques on the beach, and beach barbecues. A four-lane highway connects Aqaba with 17 kilometres of beach south of the town where more amenities are planned.

The West Bank comprises the territory beyond the Jordan River and the northern half of the Dead Sea. Since 1967 the area has been under Israeli military occupation. However the West Bank sites are not wholly lost to Jordan. Visitors can cross over and visit Jerusalem, Bethlehem and Jericho via the Allenby (now renamed the King Hussein) Bridge.

Descending to the river as it meanders from its source in Syria–in the mountain called Jebel Sheikh, the 'Old Man'–then up again through the hills of Palestine, one comes upon Jerusalem, a city of stone and light.

148

Nestling in an arm of
the Red Sea, Aqaba
offers modern air-
conditioned hotels,
sandy beaches, year-
round bathing, and a
marine life of
astonishing variety

The ancient walled city has changed little over the centuries. It still guards the sacred landmarks of the three great monotheistic faiths. On this holy ground, too, are some of man's finest architectural achievements.

Jerusalem, however, is not just a group of exceptional buildings; it is a teeming Arab city with a tangle of narrow streets. Shops and fruit stalls line the Via Dolorosa. Black-robed women grind pepper with pestle and mortar under the walls of the Holy Sepulchre. Aged Arab men play tric-trac (a game similar to backgammon) over their Turkish coffee. Laden camels and donkeys vie with mechanized means of delivery.

Within the walled courtyard of Al Haram Esh Sharif, built in AD 691 by Caliph Abdul Malik Ibn Marwan, is the third most holy shrine of Islam, the magnificent Dome of the Rock. Standing on an octagonal base, and geometrically patterned in ancient Persian tiles of lapis blue, viridian green and cream, it rises to a gold dome which is dazzling in the sunshine. The other great building within the precincts of the Haram is the Al Aqsa Mosque. And all around are other shrines and minarets.

In its 4000 years of history Jerusalem has been coveted and fought over more often than any other city. Its first occupants were probably Canaanites, and the subsequent occupants included Jebusites, Israelites, Babylonians, Persians, Seleucids, Romans, Byzantines, Omayyads, Crusaders, Mamelukes, Turks, and many others whose marks are still decipherable on the ancient buildings.

Near the Noble Sanctuary there is a small museum of Islamic treasures with inscriptions from the Koran in stone, ceramic tiles and mosaics. Outside the walled city, almost opposite Herod's Gate, the Palestine Archaeological Museum houses a wealth of history and prehistory. The exhibits include fossils, jewellery, burial urns and statuary, all chronologically arranged.

Of the many fine ancient and modern churches the most important of all is the Church of the Holy Sepulchre, Christianity's most sacred shrine. Its walls enclose four Stations of the Cross, the two most important being Calvary, in the Chapel of Golgotha, whose exquisite murals depict the nailing to the Cross and the death on the Cross, and the Tomb of Christ beneath a marble slab where a candle burns perpetually. The church is a mixture of three broad periods of construction— Byzantine, Crusader and nineteenth-century Greek.

The Via Dolorosa begins near St Stephen's Gate and winds through the city *souks*, where the faces and dress of the people must be much now as they were when Jesus climbed the narrow path bearing his cross. This hallowed way is followed by countless pilgrims tracing the fourteen Stations of the Cross that mark Christ's route. Prominent on the Via Dolorosa are the Franciscan Monastery of the Flagellation, the Convent of Notre Dames de Sion and the 'Ecce Homo' Basilica.

Also within the city walls are the Crusader Basilica of St Anne, designed in the Burgundian Romanesque style, and the gorgeously decorated Armenian Cathedral of St James, built on the site where the Apostle James was beheaded by Herod Agrippa I in AD 44.

The Citadel of Jerusalem, with its five towers, is built upon Crusader foundations. The huge fourteenth-century Mameluke fortifications, though, were renovated by Suleiman the Magnificent in 1540, and the minaret was added in 1665.

Opposite Mount Moriah, 2680 feet above sea level, the Mount of Olives affords a magnificent view of the city and, to the east, of the Dead Sea Valley. Traditionally the village of Bethphage, from which Jesus set forth on his triumphal entry into Jerusalem, is situated on the eastern reaches of the mountain. The western face is the scene of his Agony, arrest, and Ascension.

On its slopes in the Garden of Gethsemane there are ancient twisted olive trees, flower beds, and a pervading scent of rosemary. There is the Grotto where Christ's disciples slept. Nearby is the Tomb of the Virgin, or Church of the Assumption. Next to Gethsemane is the Basilica of the Agony, or Church of All Nations. Among other churches on the mount are the Russian Cathedral of St Mary Magdalene, the Dominus Flevit Chapel, the Church of the Ascension, and the Church of Pater Noster—where the Lord's Prayer is written in sixty-two languages on majolica tiled panels. Many of these churches incorporate older structures built around early Christian tombs and sepulchres.

In the Kidron Valley, lying beneath the east wall of the Old City near the Golden Gate, are a cluster of Graeco-Hasmonean tombs whose distinctive mixture of styles reflect the cultural diversity of the period. Those huge defensive city walls and their numerous gates were built in the sixteenth century by Suleiman the Magnificent.

At Bethany, less than two kilometres from Jerusalem on the road to Jericho, lived Mary and Martha, Lazarus and Simon. There is a church over the tomb where Jesus raised Lazarus from the dead. Eighteen kilometres south of Jerusalem is Bethlehem, and one of the oldest churches in the world still in use. Originally built by Queen Helena in AD 330 it marks the stable where the infant Jesus lay and the Three Wise Men came to pay homage. Other sites associated with the Nativity are the Milk Grotto and Shepherd's Field.

Fruit vendor in the *souk*,
Jerusalem
Right : Second Station of the
Cross in the Via Dolorosa. On
the right is the Church of the
Condemnation which marks the
site where Pontius Pilate
sentenced Jesus. In the background the 'Ecce Homo' Arch
spans the street. Here, according
to tradition, Pilate stood and
declared 'Behold the man!'
before pronouncing sentence

The Mount of Olives, framed by an arcade of the Dome of the Rock. The most prominent landmark is the Tower of Ascension on the skyline. The Dominus Flevit Chapel is halfway down on the right. In the foreground, left, are the gilded onion domes of the Cathedral of Saint Mary Magdalene

Hebron, south of Bethlehem, is one of the oldest Canaanite towns. It has a beautiful mosque, the Haram Al Khalil, built over the tombs of Abraham, Isaac, Jacob, Sarah, Rebecca and Leah, in the burial cave of Machpelah.

North of Jerusalem stretches the homeland of the Good Samaritan of the parable and of today's 350 surviving Samaritans. Near Nablus Jesus converted the woman of Samaria at Jacob's Well, and Joseph's tomb is in Jacob's Field. The rugged Mount Gerizim is sacred to the Samaritans, who believe themselves to be the 'chosen of God'. They have a 3000-year-old copy of the Pentateuch. In Sebastia are numerous biblical sites and relics, Herod's Temple of Augustus, and a Roman stadium and theatre.

The most famous documents to come out of these Bible lands in our time have been the Dead Sea Scrolls, found by a Bedouin shepherd boy in earthenware jars in the Qumran caves, where they had been hidden by members of the Essene sect against the threat of a Roman invasion. Qumran has since come into the tourist limelight, and the treasure it has yielded is of deep interest to people of all races and creeds.

Qumran is reached from nearby Jericho (Ariha), which lies 40 kilometres north-east of Jerusalem in the Jordan Valley, a sudden oasis in a salt encrusted landscape. Here waters from Elisha's Spring, and from springs in the Wadi Al Qilt, produce the lush landscape whose palms, vines and fruit made it such a prize even in Cleopatra's day. Jericho is at once modern, historic, ancient and prehistoric—being the oldest known inhabited city in the world. The archaeological excavations are open to the public. From Jericho one can visit the fine Omayyad palace of Khirbat Al Mafjar.

This, in brief, is what Jordan offers the visitor—a wide variety of landscapes and sight-seeing pleasures, lovingly preserved ancient beauty and first-rate modern tourist facilities. Add to that a gracious, well-educated and hospitable people whose traditions insist that every visitor be treated as an honoured guest, and a holiday in Jordan becomes an experience to be remembered.

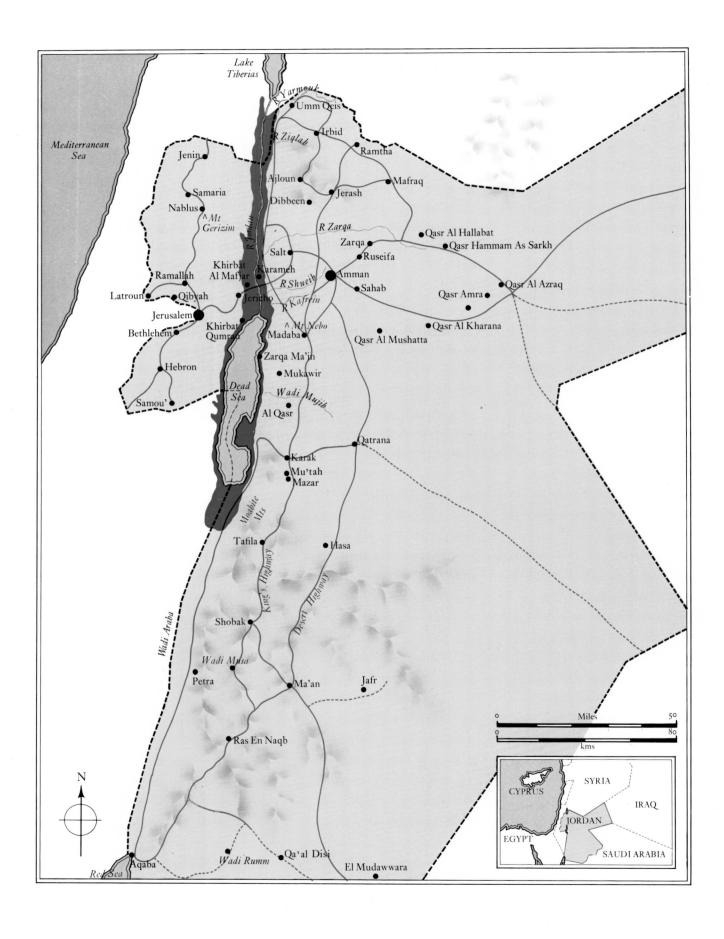

Some facts about Jordan

Capital:
Amman (population in 1979, excluding outlying suburbs, 648 587)

Government:
Constitutional Monarchy with a Parliament consisting of two houses, an Upper House or Senate appointed by the King, and a House of Representatives elected by adult suffrage. At present the task of Parliament is carried out by a National Consultative Council until new elections can be held.

Area and Population:
The total area of Jordan is 96 188 square kilometres, and the East Bank has an area of 90 309 square kilometres. The population in 1979 was 2 152 273, according to the census taken in the East Bank.

Climate:
Semi-arid: sunny days with cool nights.
Average temperature: May–October 33°C
                               November–April 14°C

Local Time:
GMT + 2 hours

Weights and Measures:
The metric system is used but a few local terms have been retained.
250 grammes = 1 uqiiya
1 000 square metres = 1 dunum

Currency:
1 000 Fils = 1 Jordanian Dinar (JD)
Amounts less than a Dinar are usually measured unofficially in terms of the Piastre (10 Fils = 1 Piastre).

National Economy at a Glance:
Gross Domestic Product at factor cost 1979*: 540.8 million JD
Gross Domestic Product at market prices 1979*: 633.8 million JD
Gross National Product at market prices 1979*: 790.8 million JD
Net National Product at market prices 1979*: 679.9 million JD
Government Expenditure 1980*: 517.6 million JD
Government Revenue 1980*: 482.0 million JD
Commodity Imports 1979: 589.5 million JD
Domestic Exports 1979: 82.5 million JD
Re-Exports 1979: 38.3 million JD
Cost of Living Index Jan. 1981 (1975 = 100): 189.4
Index of Industrial Production 1980 (1975 = 100): 232.1
Share Price Index Jan. 1981 (Jan. 1978 = 100): 154.46
(*: provisional estimate)
Source: Central Bank of Jordan

Free Zones:
There is a Free Zone at the Port of Aqaba and a joint Syrian-Jordanian Free
Zone on the border between the two countries.

Index

Numbers referring to illustrations are in italics

Acknowledgements

The publishers wish to thank the following museums, collections and agencies by whose kind permission the illustrations are reproduced. Photographers appear in italics

AID Photo, *Kay Chernush* 98 (right), 132
Aramco World Magazine, 102 (bottom left), 105 (right), 121, 122 (bottom left, right), 124
Reproduced by courtesy of The Trustees of The British Museum, 8, 14, 15, 16
Camera Press, 48 (right), 130, *William Carter* 115 (below), Crown Copyright Reserved, 87, *Wim Swaan* 22 (left), 29, 151, 152
Robert Enever Associates, *Tony Robins* 84
Susan Griggs Agency, 53 (bottom right), 148, *Kerry Johnson* 22 (right), 55 (top), *Adam Woolfit* 50, 53 (left)
Sonia Halliday Photographs, *Jane Taylor* 12, 27 (left, below right)
John Hillelson Agency, *Michael Hardy* 2, 70 (bottom left), *C. Salhani* 47 (bottom row, far right)
Reproduced by courtesy of the Jordan Information Bureau, Washington, D.C., 26, 38, 45, 47 (top row; second row, right; third row, right; bottom row, centre), 48 (left), 57, 75 (top), 82, 92, 99, 100, 111 (above), 113, 140
Keystone Press Agency, 47 (second row, left; third row, left; bottom row, left), 60, 63, 64, 70 (above right, below right), 126 (left)
Magnum Photos, *Charles Harbutt* 66, *George Rodger* 40, 68
Middle East Archive, *Alistair Duncan* 20, 30, 53 (top right), 56 (right), 72, 77, 144 (top right)
Reproduced by courtesy of the Ministry of Information, Jordan, 10, 18, 23, 24, 25, 32, 35, 52 (right), 54, 55 (bottom), 56 (left), 70 (top left), 75 (bottom), 76, 79, 80, 89 (left), 94, 97, 98 (left), 102 (top, bottom right), 105 (left), 111 (below), 115 (above), 117, 122 (above left), 129, 135, 138, 142, 144 (left, bottom right), 146, 147, 149
Reproduced by courtesy of the Ministry of Tourism, Jordan, 126 (right)
Popperfoto, 17, 27 (above right), 36, 44, 52 (left), 58, 69

CONTENTS

£6.99

YOU'VE BEEN FRAMED!

Sylvester's made 8 changes to this photo to make it look like Tweety broke Granny's vase!

Can you spot them all and get Tweety out of trouble?

Original

Changed

Writer: Bill Matheny Penciller: Horacio Saavedra Inker: Ruben Torreiro Letterer: Javier Saavedra Colorist: Prismacolor

THE NEXT AFTERNOON...

OH DEAR!

I'D BETTER HURRY OR I'LL BE LATE FOR MY SLAM DANCING LESSON!

I'LL BE BACK IN A COUPLE OF HOURS, TWEETY.

SHE'S LEAVING. NOW HAUL YOUR FLEA-BITTEN CARCASS IN THERE AND CATCH THAT BIRD! DO YOU UNDERSTAND ME?

YES, THIR, THARGE, THIR!

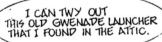

FINALLY...

THE END

TWEETY IN DISTRESS!

Sylvester's caught Tweety and is planning to serve him up in a nice Tweety soup! Can you rescue Tweety before the soup's ready?

INSTRUCTIONS:
1. The soup will be ready in 5 minutes.
2. Each time you pass through a clock symbol, you lose a minute.
3. To get to Tweety in time, find the only route that takes 5 minutes or less.

1 MIN
1 MIN
1 MIN
1 MIN
1 MIN
1 MIN
1 MIN

WB1917

THE MOUSE WAS A LOUSE

EARL KRESS — WRITER
LEO BATIC — PENCILLER
HORACIO OTTOLINI — INKER
SERGIO GARCIA — LETTERER
DAVE TANGUAY — COLORIST
DIGITAL CHAMELEON — SEPARATIONS
HARVEY RICHARDS — ASST EDITOR
JOAN HILTY — EDITOR

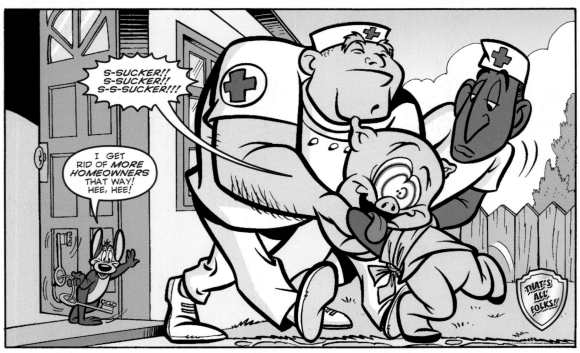

PORK SPY!

Poor Porky has a terrible headache and simply won't allow any more visitors. Except, of course, if it's Petunia Pig! Help Porky keep unwanted guests out by spotting who's who through the keyhole.

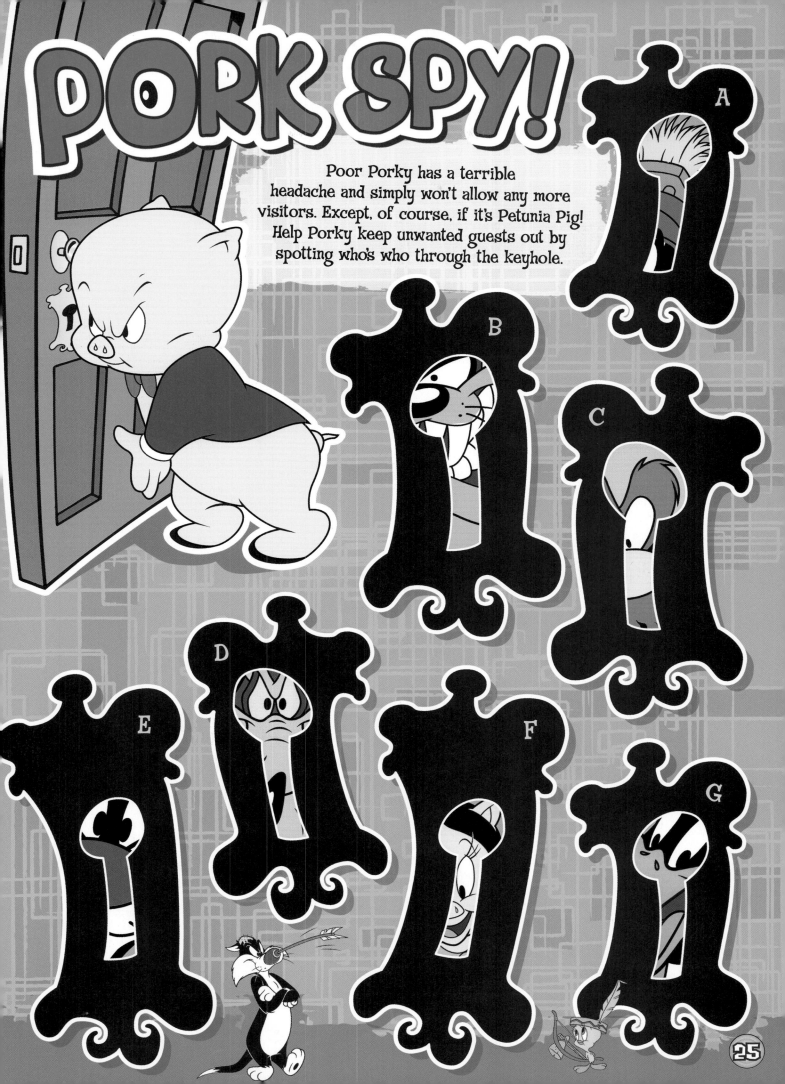

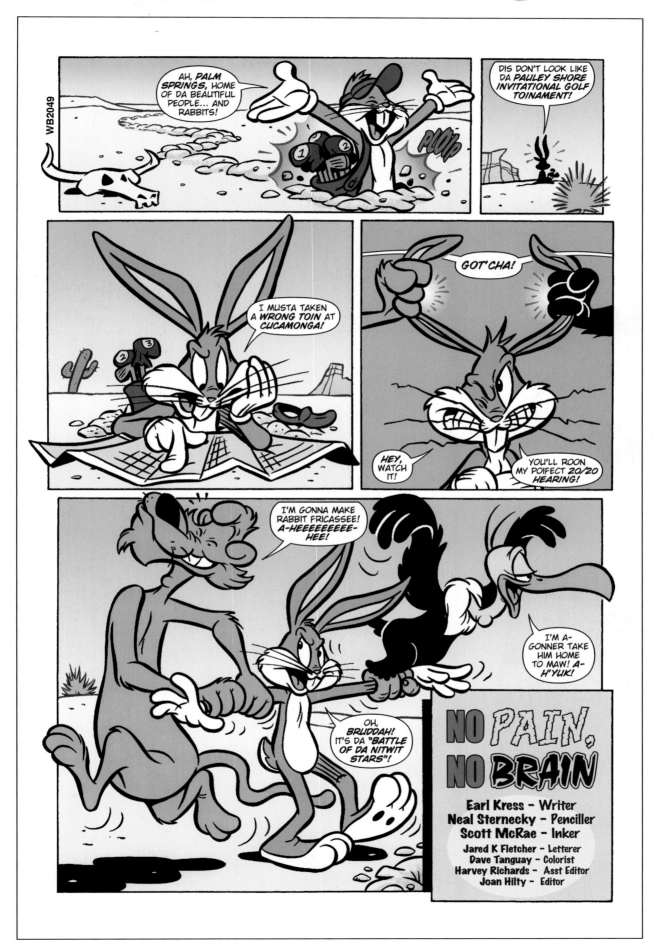

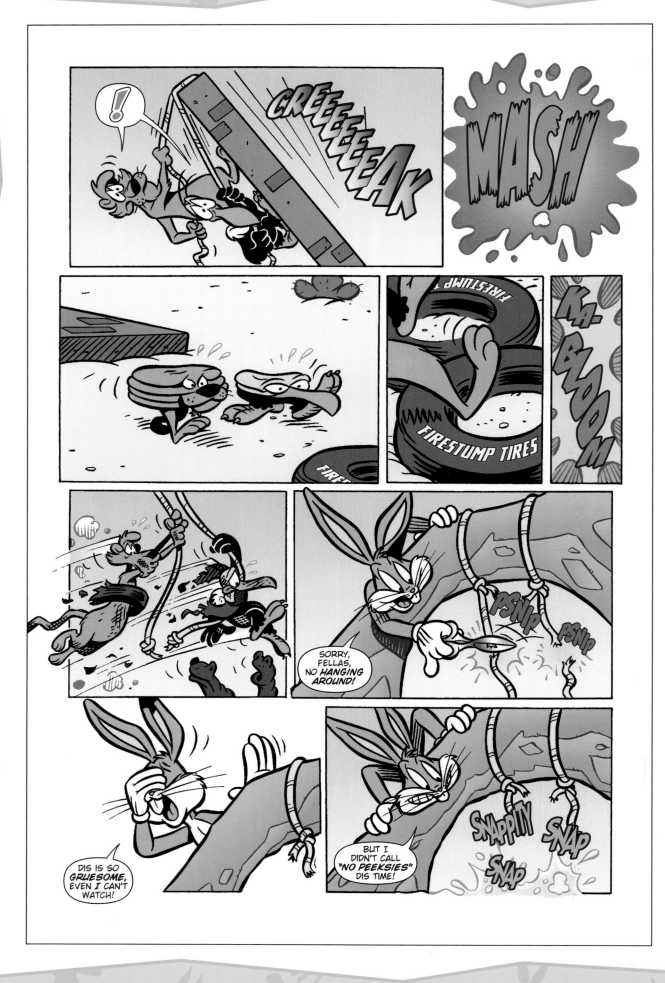

LOONEY OLYMPICS!

EVENT 3: TNT TOSS!

The aim of this event is to juggle the highest number of dynamite sticks!

Can you work out who wins?

ANSWERS ON PAGE 62

CA-TAZ-TROPHE!

Taz has started a riot at Bugs' place, and the poor old rabbit looks set to lose his prize-winning carrot collection! Help Bugs by finding all his carrots and spotting all the unwanted visitors!

Tick the boxes as you find each one.

- 10 Carrots
- Taz
- Sylvester
- Wile E Coyote
- Road Runner
- Yosemite Sam
- Elmer Fudd
- Tweety
- Porky
- Daffy
- K9

Rabbit Season

39

COUNTDOWN TO KA-BOOM!

Marvin's super planet-destroying laser has got a bit mixed up and thinks Marvin is a planet!

Help him find the shutdown password before it's too late!

INSTRUCTIONS...

1. Find and cross out all the words below.
2. Then enter the left-over letters into the empty box below to form the password.

MARTIAN
MARS
VENUS
EARTH
BEAM
K9
WAR
GALAXY
LASER
SAUCER
CONQUER
BOOM
SPACE
MARVIN

```
S M A R V I N S C C
P A B M E A R A O
A R E V N I N U N
C T A T U H M C Q
E I M E S E A E U
G A L A X Y R R E
C N O R L A S E R
N Q U T E R K 9 O
W A R H R B O O M
```

Enter left-over letters here, in reading order from top-left of grid.

40

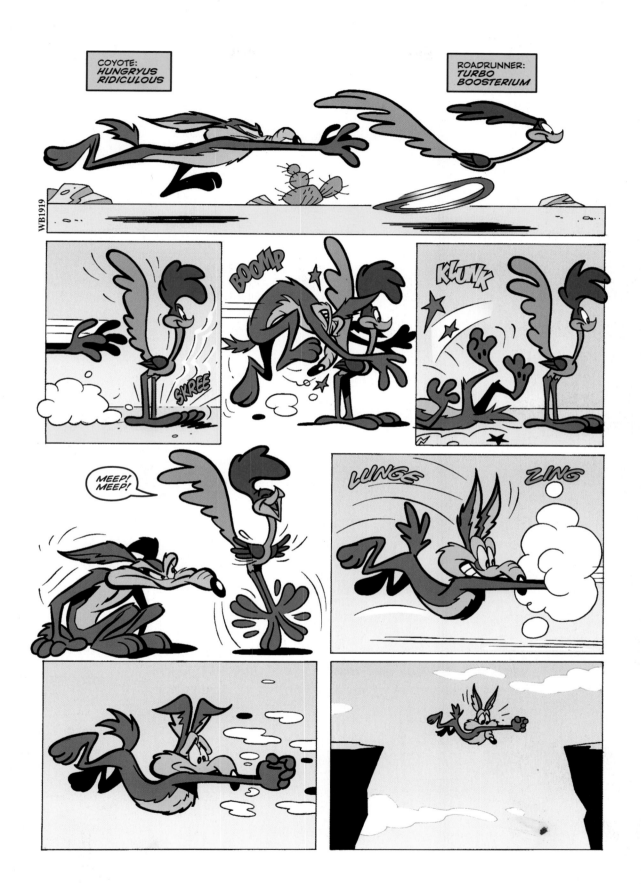

SEEING STARS

JAMES DENNING-STORY
NEAL STERNECKY-PENCILLER
JOHN BEATTY-INKER
SERGIO GARCIA-LETTERER
DAVE TANGUAY-COLORIST
DIGITAL CHAMELEON-SEPARATIONS
HARVEY RICHARDS-ASSISTANT EDITOR
JOAN HILTY-EDITOR

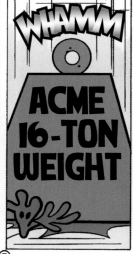

Now cover da picture with a piece of paper and twy to answer all da questions. No tweeting now pwease!

1 What colour were Wile E's running shoes?

A. Blue   B. Red    C. Pink

Tick one ☐   ☐   ☐

2 How much of his carrot had Bugs eaten?

A. Half of it ☐

B. A bite ☐

C. None of it ☐

3 How many Martians were there?

A. 2 ☐

B. 6 ☐

C. 4 ☐

4 Where was Elmer Fudd hiding?

A. Behind Wile E ☐

B. Behind a rock ☐

C. He wasn't there ☐

5 Which face was Road Runner making?

A. ☐

B. ☐

C. ☐

6 Who was peering out of the hole?

A. Marvin   B. Daffy    C. Porky

☐   ☐   ☐

7 Was K9 there?

A. Yes ☐

B. No ☐

8 Where did the scene take place?

A. The park ☐

B. Space ☐

C. The desert ☐

WANTED!

COMPLETE THE DOT TO DOT TO FIND OUT WHO'S LOONEY TUNES' MOST WANTED MANIAC!

TAZM
TOURI

ANIAN
T BOARD

**TAZMANIAN
TOURIST BOARD**

**Wanted for destroying public property,
eating public property, terrorising the
general public, and eating the general public.**

**REWARD $1,000,000,000,000,000,000,000,000,
000,000,000,000,000,000 + $1.69 expenses.**

FRANK STROM:
writer
JOHN CONSTANZA:
penciller
MIKE DeCARLO:
inker
RYAN CLINE:
letters
DAVID TANGUAY:
colors
HARVEY RICHARDS:
asst editor
JOAN HILTY:
editor

LOONEY HOLIDAY!

Tweety thought a nice trip to the beach might help everyone get along. He was wrong! Add a wave of colour to this bonkers beach scene!

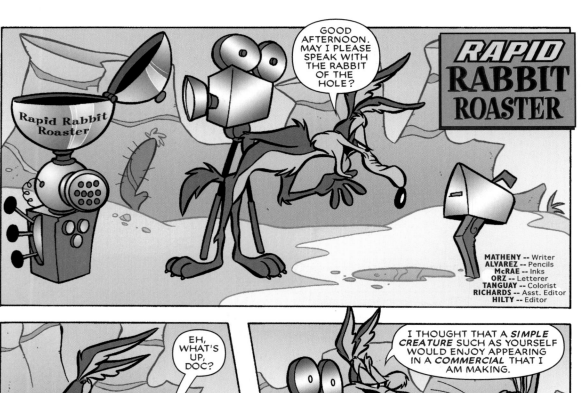

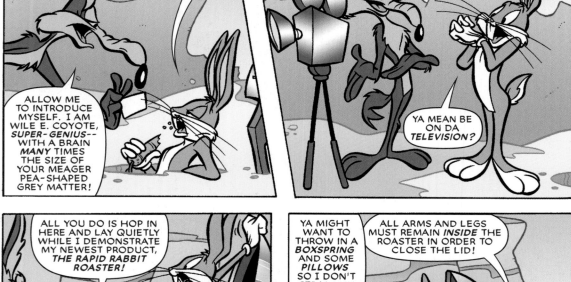

ANSWERS!

Page 15 - Let's Rumble!

The toons fighting were Taz, Sylvester, Porky, Bugs, Yosemite Sam, and Wile E Coyote

Looney Olympics!

Event 1 - Road Runner wins
Event 2 - Taz wins
Event 3 - Bugs wins
Event 4 - Daffy wins

Page 4 - You've Been Framed!

Page 25 - Pork Spy

A - Marvin, B - Taz, C - Yosemite, D - Wile E,
E - Sylvester, F - Petunia Pig, G - Daffy

Page 16 - Tweety in Distress!

Page 36 - Ca-Taz-Trophe!

Page 40 - Countdown To Ka-Boom!

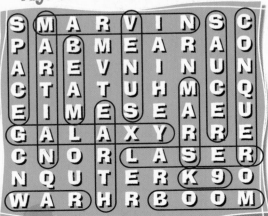

No tweeting now!

Password:
MARVIN THE CONQUEROR